THE INCREDIBLY STRANGE
HISTORY OF ECSTASY

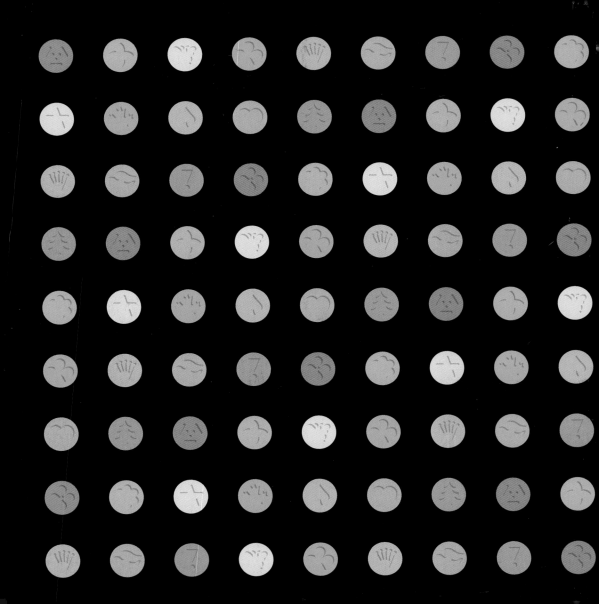

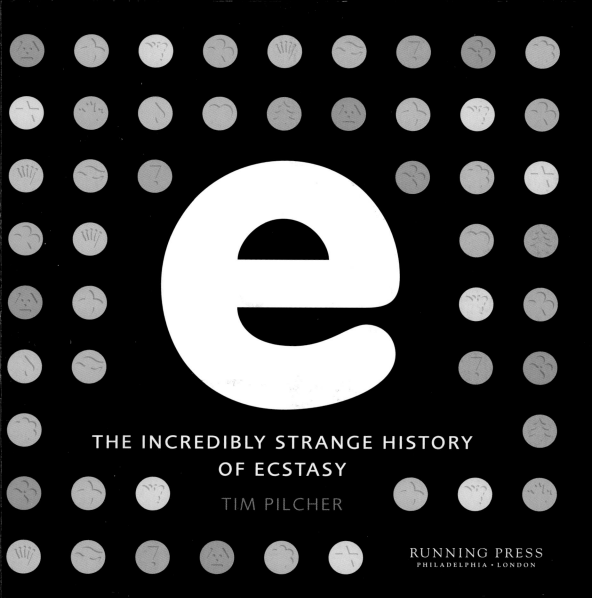

e

THE INCREDIBLY STRANGE HISTORY
OF ECSTASY

TIM PILCHER

RUNNING PRESS
PHILADELPHIA · LONDON

This 2008 edition published by Running Press, by arrangement with
Elephant Book Company Limited,
14, Dryden Court, Renfrew Road, London, SE11 4NH, United Kingdom.

9   8   7   6   5   4   3   2   1
Digit on the right indicates the number of this printing

Library of Congress Control Number: 2007923123

ISBN 978-0-7624-3184-7

Editorial Director: Will Steeds
Project Editors: Laura Ward, Chris Stone
Copyeditor: Rob Dimery
Designer: Paul Palmer-Edwards, Grade Design Consultants, London
Picture Research: Katie Greenwood
Index: Sandra Shotter
Production: Robert Paulley
Color reproduction: Modern Age Repro House Ltd, Hong Kong
Cover design by Grade Design Consultants, London

Running Press Editor: Jennifer Leczkowski

This book may be ordered by mail from the publisher.
Please include $2.50 for postage and handling.
But try your bookstore first!

Running Press Book Publishers
2300 Chestnut Street
Philadelphia, PA 19103-4371

Visit us on the web!
www.runningpress.com

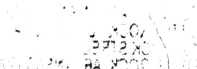

Contents

Foreword by Douglas Rushkoff

Every culture and subculture gets the drugs that it deserves. In fact, almost every major cultural movement in history can be traced back to the chemicals it did or did not have.

Rave is no exception. Whether Ecstasy proves to be emotional therapy or a long-term serotonin liability, its design and function were perfectly wed to rave culture. The poster child of designer drugs, Ecstasy was the chemical of choice for a designer psychedelic culture.

More than anything, rave was an intentionally designed experience. The music, lighting, and ambience were all fine-tuned to elicit and augment altered states of consciousness. The rhythm of the music was precisely 120 beats per minute, the frequency of the fetal heart rate, and the same beat believed to be used by South American shamans to bring their tribes into a trance state. Through dancing together, without prescribed movements, or even partners, rave dancers sought to reach group consciousness on a level they had never experienced before.

Unlike LSD, Ecstasy provided a more even plateau of duration than the highly arched LSD trip. Users took the drug and experienced its full effects in less time. Instead of rising to a crescendo and then releasing users into free fall, Ecstasy came on more subtly, gently coaxing its users into a mild and communicative euphoria. Instead of journeying inward, E users found themselves venturing outward. Ecstasy's flatter and correspondingly more predictable onset and duration made it a much more practical enhancement to an eight-hour party. Its amphetamine-like side effects helped users dance longer and with greater energy than they might otherwise, guaranteeing that they would be out on the floor with their newfound friends during the group's peak moments. No one wanted to be left out.

E immediately proved itself a carefree, social drug. Although MDMA became notorious for fostering "inappropriate bonding" in a romantic setting, it also was just as celebrated for developing group cohesion, dissolving inhibitions, and catalyzing an almost tribal sensibility. It was almost as if a group of people taking E together became empowered collectively.

It was a three-part process. First, Ecstasy stripped away the user's inhibitions to self-expression. Young men who had long repressed their feminine sides felt an irrepressible urge to express their anima, their female spirit. While a few experimented with homosexuality, it usually had less to do with defining sexual identity than with eradicating overly determined and intimacy-restricting social roles. Everyone is OK and beautiful just exactly as he or she is.

In the second stage one sought to recognize and embrace the emotional needs and personality traits of others. The third stage, most important to the group, sees the majority of the crowd soon realizing that speech and one-to-one contact is no longer a sufficient means of reaching out and accepting the thousands of other people present. That's why they turned to dance.

The peak of the E experience was when the drug and dance ritual brought the revelers into what seemed to nearly everyone to be a state of collective consciousness. Descriptions of these extended moments of group awareness often fall into cliché, but they were profound, often life-changing events for those who experienced them. The dancers achieved what can only be described as "group organism." That is, the individuals form a dynamic system like a coral reef, where each person experiences himself or herself more as a member of the collective entity than as an individuated being.

The collective formed purposefully by E-charged ravers was the result of a ritual self-consciously formed for no purpose other than the sensibility of group mind itself. The collective awareness achieved through mass MDMA use perfectly matched the social agenda of the subculture it came to serve. In their quest to find a drug capable of forging new social bonds, the rave underground happened upon a chemical that exceeded their original expectations. Ecstasy broke social inhibitions while engendering an empathic imperative that fostered new social levels of emotional bonding. Like indigenous tribes who, after ingesting various combinations of rain-forest psychotropic drugs, would dance in a group trance around the shaman's fire, ravers found their newfound tribal imperative actualized on the dance floor and catalyzed by a chemical.

Given today's widespread use of this drug, often under far less intentional circumstances, it seems appropriate that we step back and take a look at where Ecstasy came from, what its early proponents said it was supposed to be all about, and how it was integrated into popular culture—for better and for worse.

Professor Douglas Rushkoff, Ph.D, is the author of several best-selling books on culture and technology including Cyberia, Playing the Future, *and the novel* The Ecstasy Club. *He regularly contributes to* Time magazine *and the* New York Times. *His latest book is* Get Back in the Box.

A form of this foreword first appeared in Julie Holland's Ecstasy: A Complete Guide *(Park Street Press, 2001).*

Introduction

The history of Ecstasy is probably one of the most complex, confused, misunderstood, misrepresented, and emotive stories possible. Over the past 25 years, we have seen MDMA go from being praised as a serious psychotherapeutic aid, to being vilified by global governments and media, to coming full circle again with FDA-approved trials using Ecstasy to treat post-traumatic stress disorders.

In Britain, the government has admitted that the "Just Say No" tactics of the last 25 years have failed. Martin Barnes, chief executive of DrugScope, has stated, "Teenage drug use increased so much in the 80s and 90s that alarmist campaigns like 'Just Say No' lost credibility because young people knew drug users who were not coming to harm." Barnes believed the campaign prompted by the death of British girl Leah Betts (who died from drinking too much water after taking E) backfired because young people who had experimented with Ecstasy knew a tablet was very unlikely to kill them.

That said, for various reasons Ecstasy use has been in steady decline over the last ten years. Drugs naturally go in and out of fashion and today's clubbers—who were not even born when the acid house/rave movement started—prefer the likes of ketamine and crystal meth as their *drugs du jour*. Another reason for Ecstasy's relative unpopularity at the moment is the difficulty in obtaining good-quality pills. All too often, Ecstasy's nastier cousins—MDA and MDE—are sold as the real deal, constantly letting down clubbers. Because of this, the popularity of pure MDMA powder has been on the rise among older clubbers. MDMA often needs to be mixed with other chemicals to bind it into a pill, but in a powder form it can be pure. Another alternative has been the increase in so-called legal herbal Es. These are made from natural ingredients and plant combinations, and some people swear by them—though for most of them, the jury is still out. Unfortunately, it seems that as soon as a really effective legal alternative is discovered, governments immediately ban it, creating an endless battle of wits between alternative chemists and legislators.

As is so often the case with a book of this size, there simply is not the space to include everything that should be in here. The infamous 1990 "Battle of Trafalgar Square" and the UK's "poll tax" riots—both turning points for ravers' rights—have had to be sacrificed, as has the other great "battle" at Castlemorton, UK, in 1992, where free party sound systems such as DiY, Andrealin, Circus Wasp, Bedlam and many others gathered together with Spiral Tribe, and saw their illegal rave smashed up by the police.

Nor is there space to do justice to some of the groundbreaking nightclubs such as The Cross, and RIP at Clink Street. Pioneering DJs like Felix Da Housecat and Carl Cox fail to get their props here, for which

I'm truly sorry. And it'll take another book to cover the early 90s Newcastle warehouse rave scene in Sydney, Australia, and the increasing use of Ecstasy by the youth of Japan.

However, I *have* managed to squeeze in 95 years of Ecstasy history, covering everything from Alexander Shulgin's early experiments, through its use in the US nightclubs of the early 80s, to the complete transformation it caused in modern dance music. Without Ecstasy, today's multimillion-dollar clubbing and dance-music industry would not exist. The scenes in Europe and the US are explored, and the festivals, faces, freaks, and fashions are all crammed inside. Plus, there's a unique look at the myriad pill designs from over the years, as well as the art, flyers, and comics inspired by rave culture.

Look at this book as a fond scrapbook of amazing memories—if you were lucky enough to live through those crazy times. Alternatively it can act as a starting point, a signpost, to go and find out more—the bibliography lists some great books on the subject. Personally, this has been a trip down memory lane, and while I was not always at the heart of the storm, I was there in London during the heady days from 88 to 96 at Club UK, the Hyde Park Riot, and the poll tax riots in Islington. I knew Nick Coleman—fashion designer and co-founder of Solaris night; Dave Anderson—creator of Bastard Bunny—and many other of the scenesters mentioned in the book.

This book is in no way an attempt to glamorize or advocate drug use. Whether or not to use E, or any drug, is a decision that has to be made by the individual. Just remember that—as with anything in life—there are penalties that come with any rewards. Those penalties can include jail, loss of friends, family, jobs, and even life itself. But the rewards could be a new perspective on life and hopefully a less selfish, less materialistic, and more empathetic world.

Remember: keep it safe and keep it fluffy!

Tim Pilcher
Brighton, December 2007

THE HISTORY OF ECSTASY

01. The history of ecstasy

From German labs to the US military

Contrary to popular belief, Ecstasy is not a relatively new drug that first appeared in the 1980s. It was actually first synthesized almost 70 years before it became synonymous with the rave dance scene. As with LSD and many other drugs, its birthplace was a European chemistry lab.

In early 1912, German chemist Anton Köllisch was working for pharmaceutical giant Merck in Darmstadt when he inadvertently created 3,4-methylenedioxy-methamphetamine—a.k.a. methylenedioxymethamphetamine, or more simply: MDMA. Popular myth has it that Merck were trying to create an appetite suppressant at the time; in fact, Köllisch was initially endeavoring to devise a styptic (a drug intended to slow the bleeding from wounds). Merck's main rival, Bayer, had already patented a blood-clotting medicine (hydrastinine), so Köllisch was under considerable pressure to deliver a successful alternative. Convinced that a similar compound, methylhydrastinin, would be equally effective, he set about trying to create it without infringing on Bayer's patent. In the process, he accidentally produced an intermediate chemical—MDMA—for which Merck filed a patent on Christmas Eve 1912.

The patent was granted two years later, on May 16, 1914—two months before the start of World War I. Köllisch, however, was killed in the subsequent fighting (he died in September 1916), so he never appreciated the huge ramifications his work would have.

Merck were not new to introducing class A drugs to the market. After Wilhelm Adam Sertürner's isolation of morphine from opium in 1804, Merck pioneered the commercial manufacture of morphine for an expanding global market. Nearly 80 years later, the company were playing a vigorous role in the production and marketing of cocaine. Sigmund Freud, famous psychologist, cokehead, and author of *Über Coca* (1884), was an enthusiastic collaborator in Merck's coca research.

Although its patent had been filed in 1912, MDMA was not at this time tested on either animals or humans. Indeed, it seems that Merck forgot all about its drug—though it was the subject of a Polish-language scientific paper

Sigmund Freud fully endorsed Merck's cocaine research, describing the effects as ". . . Exhilaration and lasting euphoria, which in no way differs from the normal euphoria of the healthy person . . ."

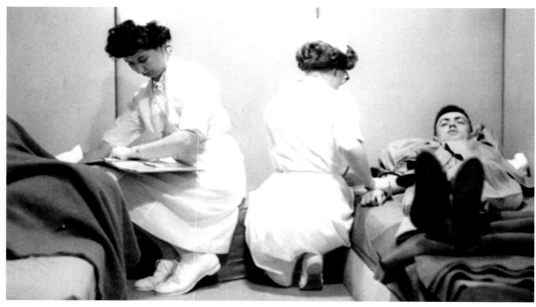

in 1924. It wasn't until 1927 that Merck carried out the first tests, on animals. Chemist Max Oberlin discovered Merck's patent and began his own work on MDMA, which he thought might have similar properties to adrenaline, as their structures were closely related. The results of his work he described as "partly remarkable," but Oberlin was forced to stop his research when the cost of the chemicals needed to make the MDMA rose sharply. ("Keep an eye on this field," he advised the company.) Merck did so; tests in 1952 revealed that the drug was poisonous to flies. Which is why you see so few of them at raves.

More controversial is the subject of the first trial tests on humans. Although no official records exist, Merck believe that one of its chemists, Wolfgang Fruhstorfer, might have carried out the first tests on humans in 1959. Not only that, but the US Air Force were carrying out secret trials of MDMA and other drugs (including MDMA's relations MDA, DMA, and MDE) in the early 50s. It is well documented that they gave enlisted men LSD, so it's possible that they popped a couple of Es in there at the same time, though no evidence has emerged to back this up. The US military used the drug in experiments in 1953, but although it is often claimed that they were searching for a truth serum at the time, the tests were actually carried out on animals, and it's more likely the authorities were looking to create new chemical weapons. Still, the image of loved-up guinea pigs and mice is a nice one. The air force gave MDMA the name EA-1475—with the EA standing for Edgewood Arsenal, where the chemicals were synthesized; the results of these studies were not declassified until 1969.

By then, others had picked up the MDMA baton and run with it. In 1970, MDMA cropped up in tablets seized by the authorities in Chicago. It was out of the lab and on the street; the genie was fully out of the bottle.

MDMA's cousin MDA

Before Ecstasy hit the nightclubs of the US, its lesser-known hippie cousin MDA had already been making the scene in San Francisco. It was first tested on humans at the New York State Psychiatric Institute in 1952 (a year before the army were blissing out monkeys with MDMA), but the experiments resulted in a particularly unfortunate incident: one of the volunteers died from an accidental overdose of 450mg, administered by the scientists.

Despite this tragic event, MDA soon made its way to the eager public—just like practically every single synthesized drug that has potential for recreational (mis)use. Known as the "the love drug" and "the mellow drug of America," MDA was making hippies smile in the Haight-Ashbury district of San Francisco throughout the 60s.

Like its more successful relation, MDA was reputed to give users heightened empathy and deeper insight, and had a buzz that lasted for anything from six to eight hours. Like LSD, it was more "trippy" than Ecstasy, though, and it is considered to be far more toxic, as has been borne out in experiments. MDA (3,4-methylenedioxyamphetamine to give it its full name) is a metabolite, or breakdown product, of MDMA and belongs to the same family of chemicals known to occur in nutmeg, mace, and sassafras. Both MDA and MDMA share the properties of amphetamine (such as speed, for example) and mind-altering drugs such as mescaline and psilocybin (magic mushrooms), but cannot be classed as either.

Despite its popularity among the communes of California, MDA never attracted anywhere near the same press attention as LSD or magic mushrooms, and its potential for inducing long "bad trips" ensured that the drug's use was comparatively limited anyway. Nevertheless, once the US government realized that people were having a good time on this new, synthesized drug, they immediately set about trying to stop them, by declaring MDA illegal—or "scheduled"—under the Controlled Substances Act of 1970.

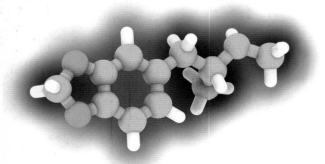

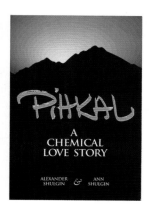

Alexander Shulgin: The Godfather of Ecstasy

In the Swinging 60s, one man was completely to revolutionize MDMA's public persona and reveal the wonder drug to the world. Born in Berkeley, California, in 1925, Dr. Alexander Shulgin was the son of Russian émigrés. He served in the US Navy during World War II, and it was during military service that he became interested in pharmacology. After the war, he studied chemistry at university and pursued a career as a psychopharmacologist, researching into the affects of drugs on the mind. In the late 50s, while completing his post-doctoral work in psychiatry and pharmacology at the University of California, San Francisco, he took mescaline for the first time. It blew his mind: "It was a day that will remain blazingly clear in my memory, and one which unquestionably confirmed the entire direction of my life," he later wrote.

After a short stint working at BioRad Laboratories, Shulgin became a senior research chemist at Dow Chemical. There, he was torn between having to produce results for his employer and his own desire to continue researching into mind-altering chemicals. Shulgin's luck changed after he managed to synthesize Zectran, the first biodegradable pesticide: Dow rewarded him with "carte blanche" research time in exchange for the highly profitable product. But Shulgin's passion for psychedelics ultimately proved too powerful a draw and he parted company with Dow in 1967, setting himself up as a freelance consultant. That same year, he first synthesized the drug he would become inextricably linked with: MDMA. When Shulgin took it for the first time, he "found it was unlike anything I had taken before . . . It was not a psychedelic in the visual or interpretive sense, but the lightness and warmth of a psychedelic was present and quite remarkable," he noted in his 1991 book, *PiHKAL: A Chemical Love Story* (a.k.a. *Phenethylamines I Have Known And Loved: A Chemical Love Story*).

Sasha, as Shulgin is affectionately known, went on to develop a new synthesis method for MDMA and began experimenting with it. He met his future wife, Ann, in 1979; a therapist, she was so impressed by Ecstasy's ability to open people up in therapy sessions that she began prescribing it to her patients. Ann and Sasha married two years later, in 1981; as with so many people after them, Ecstasy brought the two forward-thinking researchers together and bound them in love.

Deliberately shunning animal testing—which they saw as pointless, since they were examining the *human* mind—the Shulgins tried out their new synthesis on themselves. When they were satisfied it was safe, they enlisted the help of a small group of friends, who regularly tested Sasha's creations. They developed a systematic way of ranking the effects of the various drugs, known as the Shulgin Rating Scale, with a language to describe the visual, auditory, and physical sensations experienced. These early research "love-ins" were often conducted at the Shulgins' house, or at those of their friends.

In 1978, Shulgin and Dave Nichols published the first human study of MDMA, in a paper called "The Characterization of Three New Psychotomimetics [a.k.a. hallucinogens]," in which they described their subjects'—and their own—experiences as, "an easily controlled altered state of consciousness with emotional and sensual overtones." Beautiful.

"It [MDMA] takes away the feelings of self-hatred and condemnation, which are the biggest obstacles to insight . . . For reasons we don't understand, MDMA allows people to do this, typically in one [psychotherapeutic] session."

Ann Shulgin

From the couches of psychologists to the clubs of Texas

In 1976, Alexander Shulgin introduced the chemical he had synthesized to Leo Zeff, a psychologist from Oakland, California. "Actually the person who first put MDMA to work as a tool in psychotherapy was the person we call in our books Adam [Zeff], who was an elderly psychologist Sasha knew," Ann Shulgin, Sasha's wife, remembered. Zeff "tried it, and in essence, he came out of retirement, and spent the rest of his life training other therapists in Europe and in the US in the use of MDMA," recalled Ann. "He always insisted that anyone who wanted to use it with a patient should first use it on himself; that was Adam's rule, and we believe it is an excellent rule. Even if the therapist may have a quite different experience, he gets an idea of what the patient is going to feel . . ." While Shulgin has been nicknamed the Godfather of Ecstasy, Zeff has been called the Johnny Appleseed of Ecstasy because of the way he evangelized the drug. In fact, Zeff's zeal saw him introduce the substance to as many as 4,000 psychologists around the nation, according to Ann Shulgin.

DIO C'È

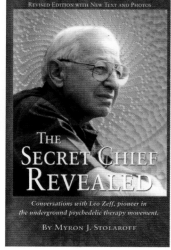

REVISED EDITION WITH NEW TEXT AND PHOTOS

THE
SECRET CHIEF
REVEALED

*Conversations with Leo Zeff, pioneer in
the underground psychedelic therapy movement.*

BY MYRON J. STOLAROFF

"I'm called the Godfather [of Ecstasy] because I published for the first time information about its effects in man. I feel content with the title. MDMA is a beautiful drug . . ."

Alexander Shulgin, 2001

"Let's face it, we're talking about elitist experience. XTC [Ecstasy] is a drug that is known, by word of mouth, by sophisticated people who sincerely want to attain a high level of self-understanding and empathy . . . No one wants a 60s situation to develop where sleazy characters hang around college dorms peddling pills they falsely call XTC to lazy thrill-seekers."

Timothy Leary, 1985

The reason the Shulgins called Zeff "Adam" was partly to protect his identity, but also because he came up with the original nickname—"Adam"—for MDMA. Zeff believed the drug stripped away a lifetime's anxieties, self-protective inhibitions, and ego defense mechanisms, returning the user metaphorically to a primordial state of innocence—akin to the biblical Adam's state before he tasted the fruit of the tree of knowledge. "I always liked [the term] Adam, because it indicates earthly paradise," wrote Dr. Claudio Naranjo, one of the first psychotherapists to see the benefits of Ecstasy's precursor, MDA, in counseling and to chart the characteristics of this and similar empathogens.

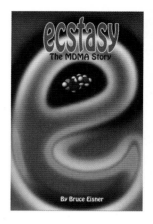

MDMA, or Adam, finally acquired its more notorious moniker, Ecstasy, via an anonymous dealer who was famously quoted in Bruce Eisner's book, *Ecstasy: The MDMA Story*, as saying, "Ecstasy was chosen for obvious reasons, because it would sell better than calling it Empathy. Empathy would be more appropriate but how many people know what that means?"

By the early 80s, word had got out to the general public about MDMA. A small group of entrepreneurs, known as the "Texas Group," saw big bucks in manufacturing and distributing the then still-legal drug. People ordered it via a toll-free phone number and paid by credit card. Over-the-counter sales were also picking up in nightclubs in Fort Worth and Dallas, and the group even paid taxes on their profits. It was estimated that the Texas Group was producing anything from 30,000 pills a month to a staggering 8,000 pills a day and possibly even as many as 2,000,000 tablets in a few months at the height of their production. And the demand was there.

The Texas Group actively marketed MDMA as a dance drug—and simultaneously, a new kind of dance music was evolving out of the dying days of disco and funk and emerging from the gay clubs. Spilling out from Chicago came house; New York had its genre-busting DJs; and Detroit brought techno to the party. These three musical influences merged with MDMA in the Texan nightclubs to become the most powerful underground youth movement seen since punk. Together, they would change everything from fashion and art to society and politics across the globe, forever.

The government decides to stop the fun—again

But the good times couldn't last. The authorities were keeping a baleful eye on the increasing use of Ecstasy in the largest state in the Union, and weren't impressed. Texan senator Lloyd Bentsen, a Democrat, wasn't happy about the happy pill in his state and urged the Drug Enforcement Agency (DEA) to make it illegal. Bentsen's quest would have tragic consequences for MDMA, just as the actions of his party-pooper predecessor, Harry J. Anslinger, had had for cannabis back in 1937.

On July 1, 1985, the DEA used recently revised legislation to place MDMA on an emergency Schedule 1 basis for a year. This meant that MDMA was rated as one of the most pernicious drugs in the US, with "no currently accepted medical use." All the psychotherapists and psychiatrists who had been using

MDMA was rated as one of the most pernicious drugs in the US, with "no currently accepted medical use."

OPPOSITE, TOP: DR. BRUCE EISNER'S 1989 BOOK, *ECSTASY: THE MDMA STORY.*
OPPOSITE, BOTTOM: A PUNK-INSPIRED FLYER FOR A LOVE RANCH RAVE, HELD IN WASHINGTON D.C. IN 1987.
RIGHT: LLOYD BENTSEN, TEXAN DEMOCRAT SENATOR WHO CAMPAIGNED TO HAVE ECSTASY OUTLAWED.
FAR RIGHT: HARRY J. ANSLINGER, FORMER HEAD OF THE DEA, WHO SUCCESSFULLY HAD CANNABIS BANNED ACROSS THE PLANET.

Ecstasy in their therapy sessions were up in arms. Led by Shulgin, Lester Grinspoon (a respected drug expert and Harvard professor emeritus), and others, the group demanded a hearing with the DEA. Oblivious to the underground use of MDMA by eminent medical professionals, the Agency was completely taken off-guard.

The lines were drawn as the arguments the DEA made against the drug—such as its potential to cause brain damage—were dismissed by the psychologists as inaccurate. (The latter argued that the DEA's test results were invalid, as they had injected their test animals with MDMA—whereas humans ingest it.) Unfortunately, however, all the data the psychiatrists had was anecdotal, as no hard scientific data had been produced regarding the effects on humans. It was a huge legal battle of "Oh, yes it is," "Oh, no it isn't." The pro-MDMA lobby still wanted to prescribe it, so they pitched for the drug to be scheduled as a level 3 drug, the equivalent of a class C status in Britain—a "controlled substance," like Valium or ketamine. The judge in the case agreed, as he could see potential medical benefits from the drug's use. Amazingly, however, he was overruled by DEA administrator John C. Lawn. Lester Grinspoon nevertheless appealed and, between December 1987 and March 1988, (a period commonly known as the "Grinspoon window") MDMA was unscheduled once more. But the naysayers of Washington D.C. were determined to prevent Ecstasy use, and on March 23, 1988, MDMA was permanently placed on Schedule 1. As such the drug was outlawed for any use whatsoever.

A bizarre rumor began to circulate, that Ecstasy could drain your spinal fluid. In fact the only way to do this is to have a surgical procedure called a lumbar puncture, which happened to research volunteers in the 80s, the possible source of the misleading tale.

RIGHT: PUBLICITY FOR THIRTIES' EXPLOITATIONAL FILMS SPREAD MUCH DISINFORMATION ABOUT CANNABIS IN THAT DECADE—A CAMPAIGN WOULD SIMILARLY BE LAUNCHED AGAINST ECSTASY, STATING THAT THE LATTER COULD CAUSE PARKINSON'S DISEASE AND "HOLES IN THE BRAIN."

The court cases brought MDMA to the media's attention, and the alarmist press began to question the safety of its use. Bizarre, and untrue, rumors began to circulate: that it could cause Parkinson's disease, or lead to a loss of spinal fluid; even that it had been responsible for the Christmas Day ceasefires of World War I. Most likely, many of these ill-informed claims were all part of the Regan-era government's propaganda machine, and its efforts to persuade Americans to "Just say 'No'" to drugs. They succeeded, in that they sowed doubt and confusion about a drug that the general public still did not really know anything about.

But for those who did understand the benefits of the drug, the prevention of all use was a bitter blow. As Ann Shulgin commented, "MDMA is penicillin for the soul; you don't give up on penicillin when you see what it can do." Yet the US government had turned its back on Ecstasy and the "Miracle Medicine/Party Drug" went underground once more.

X to E: MDMA from the US to the UK

In the early to mid-80s, regardless of the legislation, Ecstasy use was widespread across the US, and was spreading by word of mouth. Wherever people gathered to listen to the new, exciting sounds coming out of the clubs, the little pill was there—from Chicago and Detroit, to Boston and New York City. The latter would prove one of the main ports via which Ecstasy would make its way back across the Atlantic to Europe.

Many British pop stars made regular trips over to New York City to record or play, and while there they visited nightclubs such as Studio 54 and the Paradise Garage, where Ecstasy use was rife. Rising British stars such as Boy George of Culture Club and Marc Almond and Dave Bell—a.k.a. early 80s electronica duo, Soft Cell—were introduced to the happy pill by New York's glitterati elite, and it was an epiphany that would change their lives forever. Almond's experience with the Brooklyn dealer "Cindy Ecstasy" was well documented in Matthew Collins' *Altered State*: "I remember when it first hit me," the diminutive Almond recounted. "The euphoria of the first Ecstasy I ever took, and I had to go outside and I sat on the step of her apartment building,

BELOW LEFT: DAVE BELL AND MARC ALMOND, A.K.A. SOFT CELL, IN 1983. **BELOW RIGHT:** THE ECSTASY-INSPIRED ALBUM, *NON STOP ECSTATIC DANCING*, 1982. **OPPOSITE:** THE MOON SNORTING COKE FROM A SPOON IN THE DECADENT NEW YORK NIGHTCLUB, STUDIO 54.

and she came down and talked me through it. I just told her my life story and I fell totally in love with her, and we felt totally inseparable after that. It was incredible." The experience moved Almond so much, he asked Cindy Ecstasy to sing on one of Soft Cell's albums.

Boy George's experience was a bittersweet pill to swallow, so to speak. While Ecstasy opened his eyes to the world of dance music, and facilitated his budding friendship with legendary DJ Larry Levan (ultimately inspiring George himself to become a DJ), it also led the former Culture Club lead singer down the dark, murky path of drug addiction that saw him wrestle with heroin for years. "I dropped my first E among friends," he later wrote, "in a relaxed atmosphere, not in some dingy basement with a bunch of sordid dealers, although I was to meet quite a few of those in the months to come."

It was these pop stars, producers, and DJs shuttlecocking across the Atlantic that first spread the word in Britain about this new wonder drug. Ironically, Ecstasy had already been made illegal in Britain in 1977—along with all amphetamine-based drugs such as speed, MDA, and MDE—as they were believed to have no recognized therapeutic value. This "preemptive strike" against misuse took place a whole decade before the US would finally outlaw it for good. Smuggled into the country, Es were like gold dust, to the extent that British clubbers were willing to pay an extortionate (by today's standards) $50 (£25) per pill.

As in New York, the main Ecstasy users were the media and music elite—the Soho set, assorted models, journalists, designers, and pop stars. The drug was a closely guarded secret, often taken in friends' homes rather than in London's nightclubs. But it was too good a drug to remain a secret for long, and just as in America, word of mouth spread the news. In October 1985, Peter Naysmith wrote the first major article on Ecstasy to be published in Britain, for *The Face* magazine.

Although the drug was becoming increasingly popular in Britain, there was still a crucial element missing: the music. New York was already there, but it would be a few more years before Britain would discover how a very special type of music would merge with Ecstasy to become an unstoppable force for partying.

"The albums I did around that time probably wouldn't have been the same without Ecstasy. The first three Soft Cell albums— *Non Stop Erotic Cabaret, Non Stop Ecstatic Dancing,* and *The Art of Falling Apart*— were all really albums that were just done around Ecstasy and the whole E feeling."

Marc Almond

"After half an hour the drug hit me like a sensuous tidal wave. I turned into a tactile temptress and wanted to stroke the whole world. It gave me untold confidence."

Boy George

Serotonin stories:
Confessions of an Ecstasy eater

On the late Nicholas Saunders' website, Ecstasy.org, he actively encouraged users to send in their experiences, good and bad, while on Ecstasy. The counterculture guru and Neal's Yard founder also authored some of the best books about the drug, including *Ecstasy and the Dance Culture*, *E for Ecstasy*, and *Ecstasy Reconsidered*. Tragically, he was killed in an auto crash in South Africa in 1998, aged 60. But before he died, he managed to catalog numerous magical MDMA moments, including this one from "V" about her first experience on E and her relationship with her boyfriend, "S":

"The night that we took the E, I was feeling very stressed out and in a bad mood. I had told my older brother and his wife what I was planning to do, and they had some very harsh criticisms to offer, as they felt that it was dangerous . . . S had previously tried LSD and mushrooms, and both times the experience turned out to be undesirable. He struggled with family issues—the death of his father and non-closeness to anyone in his family. It was very difficult to see him ride through the emotional roller coaster. So the night we took E, I had all these thoughts on my mind. I downed the pill in frustration and anger on a completely empty stomach. When the effect started to hit me, I felt very queasy and uncomfortable. I went down in the basement to be alone and try to sort out my feelings. Everything was going wrong at this point. As a depressive person normally, I rode out these negative feelings rather than trying to turn them around.

"S came downstairs to talk to me, he was very concerned about my well-being. I didn't want to go out, but he convinced me that everything would be OK, and that he would not leave my side . . . In the car ride, I was shivering, cold and silent. I sat in the passenger seat next to S with our friends in the back. They were having a long conversation between them in the back seat, which allowed S to focus on me. He held my hand and assured me things would be OK. His smiles and confidence helped tremendously, but I still felt sick in the stomach.

"That's when S pulled out some soft electronic music—Orbital. He talked to the group about the marriage between E and house music, and persuaded them to give the music a listen. The music came on strong and overwhelmed me at first. It was the most beautiful language in the world to listen to. It spoke to me in ways no words could. It touched my heart in a way that I had never experienced before. For the first time, I truly began to appreciate S's love for this type of music.

"As the music played on, I found myself more relaxed than ever. I glanced over at S, who still held my hand firmly, and stared deeply into his eyes. I realized how much in love with him I was. He had saved me from the downward spiral I had been on. I began to talk at great length, expressing my gratitude. He was very happy to see me in such good spirits. He told me that I was the one who had changed myself, that all change comes from within . . . From that point on, I didn't want the night to end.

"The rest of the night was glorious. I grew extremely close to S, and we are still together to this day. I learned so much from the experience about myself that I am unable to express. Whenever I feel down, I put on that Orbital track, and instantly I am transported back to that magical time. The music is therapy for my soul—the best drug I could ever take, and I never want it to end. I wonder if I would have ever figured all this out without that little pill that changed my life forever?"

"The music came on strong and overwhelmed me at first. It was the most beautiful language in the world to listen to. It spoke to me in ways no words could."

Anon

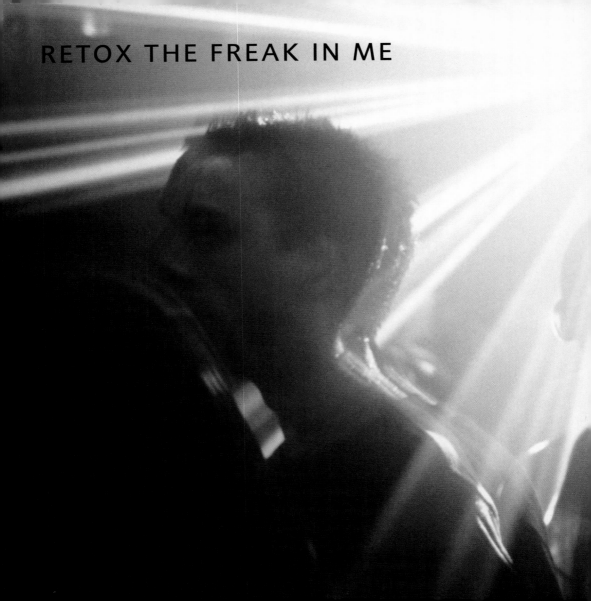

RETOX THE FREAK IN ME

02. Retox the freak in me

According to the 2005 UN World Drug Report, global Ecstasy production increased from around 141 tons in 2003 to almost 206 tons in 2004. That's a lot of pills. Professor Leslie Iversen—co-author of The Academy of Medical Sciences' study on drug reclassification in March 2007—believed that approximately 500,000 young people routinely took Ecstasy every weekend in Britain. That's almost 1 percent of the entire population of the country! Despite recent drops in consumption, the world's single largest Ecstasy market remains the United States. So why do so many people pop those funny little pills on a Saturday night? Is it the physical buzz? The feelings and emotions it unleashes? Or could it be something deeper, and more spiritual?

The physical effects of E

Regardless of the psychological effects of the drug—the reason most people take it—Ecstasy physically does many interesting and unique things to the human brain and body.

Once taken, the effects of the drug are first felt after a period of some 30 minutes to an hour. Alexander Shulgin and David Nichols' groundbreaking 1978 paper noted that the effects were very rapid, kicking in after about half an hour and wearing off after about two hours, but that was using extremely pure MDMA, something most users find almost impossible to obtain today. With most street pills, it can take anything from 45 minutes to an hour and a half before the user feels any buzz.

Impatience has led to the downfall of many a clubber. Waiting for the first pill to kick in, they pop another, as documented in The Streets' track "Blinded by the Lights": "Still not feeling anything, this one's gotta be a dud . . . Belly's not even tingling . . . I'm gonna do another I think, Yeah, one more. These are shit . . ." Then the Ecstasy takes hold, ". . . And I'm thinking, maybe I shouldn't have done the second one . . . I'm tripping out . . . Ooh, I'm maasshed." Often the first feeling a user has is a tingling sensation, with butterflies in the stomach—a jittery sensation—and increased awareness of sight, sound,

Usually, overwhelming feelings of happiness and well-being take over, and it is difficult not to smile.

and touch. Usually, overwhelming feelings of happiness and well-being take over, and it is difficult not to smile.

The way MDMA actually affects the brain, in the physical sense, is relatively simple. The brain functions by means of nerves (neurons) that connect and pass signals—either electrically or chemically—through synaptic gaps between them. One of the chemicals—known as neurotransmitters—that transports messages is serotonin (5-hydroxytryptamine, or 5-HT). Ecstasy acts by "blocking" or stopping serotonin from attaching to neurons, but uniquely it also removes serotonin from neurons it has already attached to. It then causes the brain to create massive build-ups of serotonin in the synaptic gap, which then floods the brain with the joyful "loved-up" feeling. Interestingly, MDMA affects the same serotonin receptors (5-HT2) that psychedelics, such as LSD, latch on to. This means that Ecstasy has mild psychedelic properties, but without the hallucinations—an almost unique trait. Many first-time users have experienced slight visual distortions, such as seeing "sparkly" effects on lights, as though seen through a starlight filter, or imagined tattoos on friends' faces or bodies.

RIGHT: A COMPUTER-GENERATED IMAGE OF A NEURON—ONE OF THE CELLS IN THE NERVOUS SYSTEM THAT TRANSMIT AND PROCESS INFORMATION ELECTROCHEMICALLY. THE HUMAN BRAIN HAS SOME 100 BILLION NEURONS.
FAR RIGHT: CLOSE-UP OF RECEPTORS, THE PROTEINS ON THE NEURON CELL MEMBRANE THAT INITIATE THE NEURON'S RESPONSE TO MESSAGES IT RECEIVES, BY MEDIATING THE EFFECTS OF SEROTONIN ON NEURONS, 5H-T RECEPTORS TRIGGER THE HIGHS AND LOWS EXPERIENCED BY MDMA USERS.

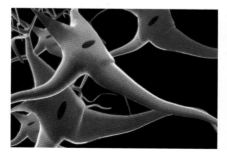

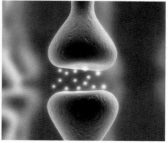

LEFT: VARIOUS VISUAL DISTORTIONS SUCH AS LIGHT TRAILS CAN BE CAUSED BY MDMA AND ITS FAMILY OF DRUGS. OPPOSITE, RIGHT: IT'S NOTHING SEXUAL, JUST SENSATION SEEKING; THE "HUG DRUG" LIVES UP TO ITS NAME. OPPOSITE, FAR RIGHT: IT'S IMPORTANT THAT ECSTASY USERS STAY HYDRATED, AND LOOK OUT FOR EACH OTHER, MAKING SURE EVERYONE HAS ENOUGH TO DRINK.

All of this backs up Ecstasy's placement in the same chemical family as mescaline. MDMA also affects the brain's other naturally occurring "happy drug," dopamine (DA), in much the same way, though to a lesser extent.

MDMA raises a person's blood pressure, increases the pulse rate, and causes the pupils to dilate heavily—in fact, users are easy to spot by their huge, black pupils. Like many amphetamines, MDMA tends to suppress appetite, and reflexes in deep-muscle tendons are enhanced; some users have difficulty walking (known as ataxia) as their muscles relax.

The majority of Ecstasy's physical side effects are well known to any raver: restlessness, hot and cold sweats, and jaw ache—another classic symptom of most amphetamines, and MDMA is no exception. In fact, in many cases excessive, uncontrollable jaw gnashing is so common that several packs of chewing gum have become an essential part of any raver's kit, along with bottles of water. Apart from the teeth-gnashing, users are more acutely aware of their senses. Hypersensitivity of the skin causes users to become extremely tactile, reveling in the sensation of touch, hence one of Ecstasy's nicknames: "the hug drug."

After heavy use, ravers sometimes complain of muscle ache and exhaustion—which is unsurprising, if you have been dancing non-stop for six hours with nothing but water for fuel. Many clubbers often find the best physical and psychological cure after a night out on Ecstasy is the simplest: decamp to a friend's home and chill out for a further 24 hours watching DVDs, eating fruit and chocolate, and drinking water and isotonic sports drinks.

The biggest risk for poppers of Es at raves is excessive dehydration and overheating, known as hyperthermia. MDMA naturally increases body temperature (which is normally 98.6°F (37°C)), and when this slightly raised

Hypersensitivity of the skin causes users to become extremely tactile and uninhibited, causing concern that some US clubbers may engage in "inappropriate" sexual behavior at raves.

temperature is further increased by prolonged dancing, lack of water, and the hot, sweaty environment of a nightclub, the combination can be deadly. If the body's temperature goes over 40°C (104°F), hyperthermia kicks in, causing seizures and convulsions. If its temperature rises above 42°C (107.6°F), organ failure and brain damage can occur, with fatal consequences. In the early 1990s, the British press widely covered several alleged Ecstasy-induced deaths, giving disproportionate column inches to relatively few tragedies. But it should be noted that hyperthermia is not caused solely by Ecstasy usage. In clinical studies, users who took MDMA in calm, cool environments, and who remained reasonably inactive, experienced only a marginal increase in body temperature. In fact, it is the activities associated with Ecstasy use—that follow the actual taking of the drug—that cause hyperthermia, not the drug itself. That is, dancing continuously for hours in an overheated room while failing to drink sufficient water to allow the body to sweat.

OPPOSITE: WATER, WATER EVERYWHERE, BUT NOT TOO MUCH TO DRINK. HYPONATREMIA (EXCESSIVE WATER INTAKE) CAN BE AS DANGEROUS AS TOO LITTLE.
RIGHT: THIS SIGN FROM THE TAIWANESE GOVERNMENT WARNS OF THE DANGERS OF ECSTASY USE.
FAR RIGHT: ECSTASY PILLS BEING TESTED FOR PURITY IN BRITAIN IN THE 1990S.

Ironically, drinking too much water can actually be as dangerous as drinking too little. Hyponatremia is a deadly flip side of the coin, when sodium (salt) levels in the blood are watered down to lethal levels. Excessive water drinkers, who consume 0.5–0.7 gallons (2–3l) in a short space of time without sweating or going to the toilet, effectively "drown" themselves. The most famous case of this rare condition was that of 18-year-old British girl, Leah Betts. In 1995, she collapsed in a coma after taking one Ecstasy tablet at her birthday party, and died a few days later. Initially the police mistakenly attributed her death to "a contaminated batch" of Ecstasy. However, the subsequent inquest revealed that Leah had drunk a staggering 1.85 gallons (7l) of water in less than 90 minutes, causing her brain to swell and hyponatremia to take hold. Leah Betts became the poster child for a huge, ten-year-long anti-Ecstasy campaign, led by her parents, under the slogan: "Sorted: Just one Ecstasy tablet took Leah Betts."

"Ecstasy stripped away the user's inhibitions to self-expression. On E, lies are inefficient, and the peculiarities or weaknesses they are meant to obscure no longer seem like offenses against nature."

Professor Douglas Rushkoff

"For a while I took Ecstasy when it was not very available over here. I took it simply because it made me feel that everything was wonderful."

George Michael

Regardless of the downsides and the mass media's rampant disinformation campaign, the truth is that Ecstasy is a relatively benign drug, in comparison to other—legal—drugs. In 1998, alcohol was responsible for 110,000 deaths in the US, tobacco killed 400,000, and even aspirin and other over-the-counter painkillers claimed 7,600 lives. And the figures for alcohol-related deaths have been steadily increasing, year after year. How many deaths were attributed to Ecstasy that year? Nine. In fact, the risk of death from taking MDMA is between 1 in 650,000 and 1 in 3,000,000—statistics the media do not broadcast very often.

The psychological effects of E

In terms of its effects on the mind, the letter "E" can stand for many traits of MDMA, including "euphoria," "ecstasy," and "empathy." It's this last one that is the most powerful reason why ravers take it. The drug enables users to feel they completely understand, and can relate to, another person's emotional state, which in turn helps to bring both people closer together. This is the real "magic" of Ecstasy. Indeed, the late author and researcher Nicholas Saunders

LEFT: MDMA'S EMPATHIC QUALITIES CAN LEAD TO LITERALLY TRYING TO GET INSIDE EACH OTHER'S MINDS.

OPPOSITE, LEFT: IN THE 1970S AND 80S, BEFORE MDMA WAS IN WIDESPREAD USE, SOCCER HOOLIGANISM WAS FUELED BY ALCOHOL.

OPPOSITE, RIGHT: WHEN MDMA HIT THE STREETS THE WORKING CLASSES LEFT THE SOCCER STADIUMS FOR THE WAREHOUSE RAVES AND SUBSTITUTED MINDLESS DANCING AND HUGGING FOR MINDLESS VIOLENCE.

suggested that E was a main cause of the reduction in soccer hooliganism in Britain in recent years. As more and more "yobs" discovered the drug in the 1990s the mass brawls between gangs at soccer matches declined markedly, as both sides realized that they didn't want to fight, but to hug! The happy pill was doing what it does best. This empathy, that fosters feelings of group belonging, is extremely primal, as is dancing to the strong repetitive beats of dance music, reminiscent of tribal drums. As the lyrics to Freakpower's single "No Way" explain, it's all about ". . . Being just a part of one big famil-E."

But Ecstasy causes people to lose fear too, as George Greer and Requa Tolbert reported in their snappily titled 1990 paper *Ecstasy: The Clinical, Pharmacological and Neurotoxicological Effects of the Drug MDMA.* "In the right circumstances, MDMA reduces or sometimes eliminates the neurophysiological fear response to a perceived threat to one's emotional integrity . . . With a barrier of fear removed, a loving and forgiving awareness seemed to occur quite naturally and spontaneously." With the fear gone, people are much more free to speak and tend to verbalize all the minutiae

in their brains in an almost stream-of-consciousness expunging of mental detritus—no matter how facile or embarrassing this might seem later on. It's no surprise that a favorite chant in the clubs was to "Keep it mental!"

Interestingly, unlike substances that create altered states of mind, such as alcohol and LSD, Ecstasy allows for completely lucid recall of the trip. As Ann Shulgin pointed out, "There is no amnesia for the event. Also, there is never any loss of control, which is probably the main unconscious fear that most people have in taking any drug that affects the mental processes."

But some users want that little bit extra—or are just never satisfied—and take both MDMA and LSD simultaneously—an experience known as "candy flipping." The result apparently mellows the acid trip without eliminating the hallucinogens. Usually the LSD is taken first followed by the MDMA, which often resparks the visual hallucinogens, and the empathic qualities of Ecstasy mix well with acid to create a "psychedelic brandy." Other, more adventurous psychonauts mix magic mushrooms and MDMA, creating what is known as an "MX Missile."

But as with most mind-altering substances, there can be a psychological price to pay. Excessive users suffer from downsides such as depression, confusion, and anxiety. These side effects are mostly caused by the reduced levels of serotonin in the brain. After the initial surge of the brain's happy drug, it simply cannot keep up production and the baseline of the serotonin drops dramatically, leaving users with that shivery, six-in-the-morning "downer" feeling. Depending on the amount of MDMA taken, this feeling can last anything from a few hours to three days, which can leave users suffering from mid-week blues. Heavy users have been known to ride an emotional roller coaster of low "mid-week hangovers" and euphoric Saturdays, and back again. Invariably it's a habit that cannot be maintained for long.

In controlled therapeutic conditions, these psychological highs and lows are rare and research is continuing into how MDMA can help deeply troubled minds. In the early 2000s, the US Food and Drug Administration (FDA) took almost unprecedented action by allowing the first legal, clinical trials of MDMA in nearly 15 years, to see if the drug could be used to help people suffering from post-traumatic stress disorder (PTSD). PTSD can occur following the experience (or witnessing) of life-threatening events such as military combat,

OPPOSITE: A HAPPY CLUBBER REVELS IN THE PROSPECT OF POPPING AN E. HOWEVER, WHILE THE HIGHS ARE UNDOUBTEDLY EUPHORIC, THE LOWS CAN LAST FOR DAYS, ESPECIALLY IN THE CASE OF LONG-TERM USERS.

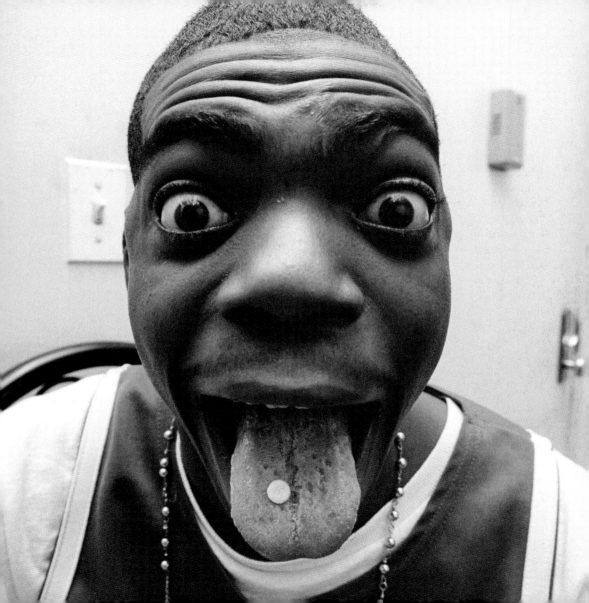

natural disasters, or violent personal assaults. Sufferers often relive the experience through nightmares and flashbacks, have difficulty sleeping, and feel detached or estranged—all experiences that can seriously disrupt their lives. In an effort to help traumatized US military personnel returning from Iraq, and victims of rape and sexual abuse—for whom existing treatments are ineffective—the FDA gave permission for them to be included in an experiment to see if MDMA can treat PTSD.

Michael Mithoefer, the psychiatrist leading a 2005 trial in South Carolina, thought the drug could help the soldiers discuss their experiences with therapists, by opening them up to talk about their traumas without fear. Mithoefer believed that the ongoing trial was, ". . . Looking very promising. It's too early to draw any conclusions, but in these treatment-resistant people so far the results are encouraging. People are able to connect more deeply on an emotional level with the fact they are safe now." The studies involved approximately 230 people, none of whom have had any serious adverse reactions. Neuropsychological tests and position emission tomography (PET) scans of the subjects' brains also provided no evidence of brain toxicity. There are also several trials concurrently running in Europe using doses similar to those in the US trials (100mg to 125mg of MDMA—the amount of an average street Ecstasy pill). All this harks back to Leo Zeff's legion of psychiatrists prescribing Ecstasy in the late 70s. It looks as if MDMA may be coming off the dance floor, and back home to the psychiatrist's couch, once again.

The spiritual effects of E

Many people relate to Ecstasy use as a spiritual experience, rather uniquely for a widespread recreational drug. Most tend to talk about the drug's ability to open what Hindus refer to as the heart chakra—that is, it makes users open to love, (and to being loved) unconditionally, without fear of repercussions. Users have experienced a knotted feeling in their chests that has "unraveled" as they let go of their feelings of tension and stress while, simultaneously, feeling as if their interpersonal relationships have healed.

Before his death, Nicholas Saunders investigated this area of Ecstasy use in particular, interviewing a wide range of people, from Benedictine monks to Zen

Buddhist masters. Nearly all concurred that MDMA actually helped students on the road to enlightenment, by opening themselves up to all possibilities. As one Zen master commented in Saunders' 1995 book, "Ecstasy is a wonderful tool for teaching. For example, I had a very keen student who never succeeded in meditation until Ecstasy removed the [mental] block caused by his effort . . ."

Saunders even took the 70-year-old Zen Buddhist monk to a British rave, he revealed in an interview. "He said that although he had a bad back and couldn't dance, he was very curious to see Ecstasy used in a rave environment," Saunders noted, "as he was only familiar with its effects in a private, spiritual context. At first, he couldn't stand the music and put his fingers in his ears. But later, I noticed his face was glowing. He was so excited. He said, 'I can see what it's all about, this is walking meditation, these people are meditating only they don't realize it. It's the same state of being completely in the here and now, although it manifests in this repetitive physical movement.'"

BELOW: SAUNDERS' BOOK, IN SEARCH OF THE ULTIMATE HIGH, ASSESSES THE ROLE OF PSYCHOACTIVES, LIKE MDMA, IN ACHIEVING A SPIRITUAL EXPERIENCE.
BELOW, RIGHT: MANY BELIEVE THAT YOGA, MEDITATION, AND OTHER "ALTERNATIVE" PRACTICES CAN BE ENHANCED WITH THE USE OF MDMA.

Numerous meditation teachers have expressed similar feelings, pointing out that Ecstasy allows the barriers between mind, body, and spirit to merge in unity, so that true enlightenment can be achieved. Other anecdotal experiences suggest that people feel properly present and no longer "distant" or "detached" from their environment or even their own bodies.

Many therapists and practitioners use the term "sacramental" when referring to the consumption of Ecstasy, likening it to a Native American's process of healing the body, problem solving, and raising spiritual awareness in a unified process; an holistic approach. In this context, Ecstasy is not taken at a club with a group of friends on a Saturday night, but rather in a "sacred space."

Often in these settings, users prepare by asking themselves what they would like out of the session. They could, for example, choose to examine any past trauma or unresolved conflicts that are troubling them. Clothes are usually comfortable and loose, and there is space to lie down or move around, with blankets available to guard from chills. Once the mind is clear and relaxed and a safe, calm environment established, a standard MDMA dose of around 150mg is usually taken. This takes some 30 minutes to take effect; the guide or therapist's demeanor is crucial at this time, as it can affect the user's mindset.

One common spiritual experience that users undergo, particularly when Ecstasy is taken outdoors, is a feeling of oneness with the natural world. People feel closer to the earth, to the plants, flowers, and wildlife around them. On a grander scale, they may experience a strong sense of belonging in the universe, a realization that everything is interconnected. Rather than promoting an overpowering feeling of insignificance or fear, this can be a comforting and empowering sensation.

Often, first-time users go through deep and profound mental and spiritual transitions. Old fears and repressions are shrugged off, people are able to express themselves openly and honestly, whereas previously they would have felt embarrassed or constrained by social judgments. Interestingly, this liberated feeling often remains with the user long after the MDMA has worn off, bringing a lasting and beneficial impact to his or her life.

Some users need only take Ecstasy once to have a profound, life-changing experience; others may need two or three sessions. Once taken, however,

OPPOSITE, LEFT: DR. JULIE HOLLAND'S COMPREHENSIVE TOME, ECSTASY: THE COMPLETE GUIDE MAKES A VERY GOOD CASE FOR THE MEDICAL USE OF MDMA. OPPOSITE, RIGHT: TEACHER, VISIONARY, FREE THINKER, AND AUTHOR OF ECSTASY CLUB, PROFESSOR DOUGLAS RUSHKOFF.

ECSTASY: THE COMPLETE GUIDE

A COMPREHENSIVE LOOK AT THE RISKS AND BENEFITS OF MDMA

EDITED BY JULIE HOLLAND, M.D.

With contributions by Andrew Weil, Ralph Metzner, Rick Doblin, Douglas Rushkoff, Sasha & Ann Shulgin, Rabbi Zalman Schachter, and others

the feeling can be recalled at anytime at will, allowing the user purposely to have a "flashback" and recall those empathic feelings. Listening to any music the user associates with a previous MDMA session can also bring on this feeling. Another spiritual effect is what users often refer to as a "contact high." If someone hasn't taken Ecstasy in a particular session—but is surrounded by those who have—they can still experience a mild form of MDMA symptoms simply by being in the proximity of those who have—the empathic link opening this gateway to the soul.

Other transformations can include changes in physical symptoms, work habits, improved relationships, shifts in the user's world view and major spiritual awakenings. Rabbi Zalman Schachter described it best in Julie Holland's 2001 book, *Ecstasy: The Complete Guide*—"When God saw that people, instead of turning to God, were turning to the medicine cabinet, God made himself available in the medicine cabinet."

"I've done 12 in one night, you know what I mean—loads of them . . . Really, in the long run, it's a safe pill and it ain't doing you no harm. I don't see the problem."

Brian Harvey, former member of British "boyband," East 17

"We're not threatened by people anymore. All our insecurities have evaporated. We're in the clouds now. We're wide open. We're spacemen orbiting the Earth. The world looks beautiful from here, man. We're nympholeptics, desiring for the unobtainable. We risk sanity for moments of temporary enlightenment. So many ideas. So little memory. The last thought killed by anticipation of the next. We embrace an overwhelming feeling of love. We flow in unison. We're together. I wish this was real. We want a universal level of togetherness, where we're comfortable with everyone. We're in rhythm. Part of a movement. A movement to escape. We wave goodbye. Ultimately, we just want to be happy. Heh, yeah . . . Hang on, what the fuck was I just talking about?"

Jip in the 1999 movie *Human Traffic*

Serotonin stories:
Agony on Ecstasy

Ecstasy, like nearly every psychoactive drug known to man, works on what Timothy Leary called, "Set and setting," that is, the state of mind of the user and the environment they're in. Here's one anonymous British clubber's tale of how the setting changed his experience:

"I remember my first time out clubbing on E. Up until then I'd only ever taken it at a friend's house, listening to chilled ambient stuff like Orbital or Underworld's classic, *Dubnobasswithmyheadman* album. I still get goose pimples listening to 'Cowgirl.' It was always a fantastic experience.

"Anyway, so a whole gang of us—about eight or ten of us—decided to check out Club UK in Wandsworth, London. This was in 1994/1995, when it was at its peak and the legendary Final Frontier on a Friday night was running. Virtually everyone DJ'ed there, including Paul Oakenfold, Andrew Weatherall, Sven Vath, and Moby. The place soon got a mad rep for major Ecstasy deals. It was so blatant; dealers were walking around shouting out, 'Pills, Ecstasy!'

"It was a freezing night and we had to climb, what seemed like, a thousand steps to get in, but going in was like entering Wonderland. We got there late and everything was already kicking off. The lightshows, lasers, and people all annihilated my senses! And the heat was incredible! Everyone was stripping down to stay cool. The club was selling small bottles of 'Club UK' water at £1.50, the same price as a vodka and orange!

"Then the E kicked in and I was off! Big smiles all round. Somehow we all got split up and I found myself alone, wandering aimlessly looking for my mates. Everyone I saw was my best friend, until I got up close to them and realized that I didn't know them.

"Then something happened. Maybe it was because I was in a big crowd on my own, feeling vulnerable, but something changed. The music started getting harder and faster, making my heartbeat increase. As the bpms started cranking up, the crowd suddenly changed from being lovely and friendly to dodgy and menacing. I was starting to freak out. I'd never had a bad time on E before and

I was starting to go into a major panic attack. I staggered into the chill-out room to calm down. I bumped into some of the gang and crashed into a giant beanbag. After a while I started feeling better, so I decided to brave the dance floor once more, but as soon as I got out there the fear gripped me again. Two mates, Paula and Eric, realized I was freaking and decided to take me home.

"Back in the taxi I was suddenly fine and all 'Wha-hey, let's go back!' but my mates knew better and we went home and chilled. It was so wonderful they looked after me; I owe them a lot, as it could've got real bad.

"Shortly after we'd been to Club UK, there was a death at the club and the police came down hard on the place with constant raids, until it had to shut.

"So my first experience of doing Ecstasy in a club had all the best, and worst, bits of an E experience mixed together. The euphoria, loved-up feeling mixed with the full-on paranoia of a bad trip, but having said that, I'm glad it happened as it made me respect the drug more and I never had a bad time after that."

"As the bpms started cranking up, the crowd suddenly changed from being lovely and friendly to dodgy and menacing."

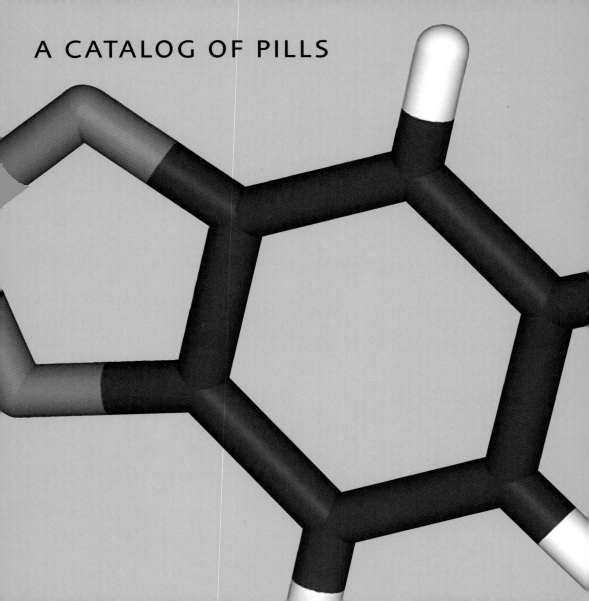

A CATALOG OF PILLS

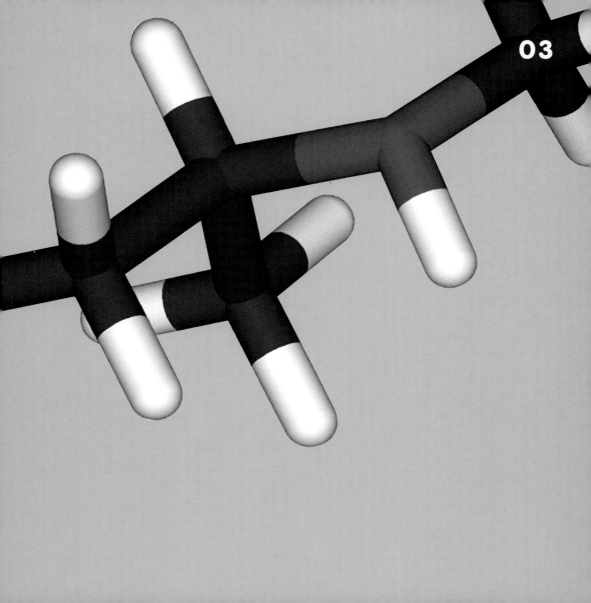

03. A catalog of pills

In the Second Summer of Love (which in fact occurred over two summers—those of 1988 and 1989), Ecstasy pills began to appear with small logos stamped on them. The logos referred to a wide range of cultural influences, from clothing designers and cartoon characters to auto manufacturers and corporate logos. These "brands" helped users identify which ones were good, bad, or just plain "rank." Brands would fall in and out of favor and dealers and manufacturers would constantly adapt and change to keep pace with demand. As the market grew, and as more and more pills began to be cut with less and less MDMA, these identifiers became crucial as a guide to quality and purity. This visual directory catalogs just some of the many types found in different countries around the world.

Today, Ecstasy pills can be cut with anything from talcum powder to caffeine; sometimes, they contain only ordinary amphetamine. In January 1998, Nicholas Saunders' organization Ecstasy.org found that only 6 out of 35 pills it tested contained MDMA, and even then these 6 only contained some 70mg, instead of the expected 100–125mg, of MDMA. Twenty-seven pills—nearly three-quarters of the total— contained speed: caffeine, amphetamine, and methamphetamine.

It was a similar story in Holland. Dutch government testing of street Ecstasy consistently discovered that as little as 60 percent of the pills tested contained MDMA. In January 1998, a drastic drop occurred: they found a reasonably active dose of MDMA in only 20 percent of pills tested.

Throughout the 90s, several aspects of Ecstasy consumption changed. Until 1991, Ecstasy meant MDMA, but afterward pill brands such as "Snowballs" started to appear, containing the old hippie favorite MDA. Other substitutes such as MDEA and MBDB began appearing after 1993, but as the effects were similar to MDMA, most clubbers didn't even notice.

In 1998 in Britain, around 10 percent of Ecstasy pills tested proved fake, containing instead aspirin, paracetamol, or other substances that had no effect. Another 5 percent contained active drugs such as amphetamine, ephedrine, and caffeine, sometimes mixed with other active drugs such as pseudo ethedrine, codeine, and dihydracodeine. The remaining 85 percent of pills tested were Ecstasy-type drugs, but only 60 percent were MDMA (the real thing); the rest were MDEA (20 percent) and MBDB (10 percent).

Some pills that have been sold as Ecstasy are in fact dextromethorphan (DXM). This sometimes means that when clubbers don't experience the buzz they are after, they then take some MDMA to top it up. The combined mix can cause serotonin syndrome—an excessive build-up of the chemical in the brain—which can result in muscle spasms, diarrhea, agitation, fear, shivering, and sweating. This has led to the idea of "smacky" Es, as the symptoms are similar to those experienced when coming down from heroin. However, substitute Es such as DXM are rarely mixed with other drugs and heroin has never been found in samples sold as Ecstasy, apart from inactive trace elements.

The dealers' greed finally came home to roost, however, when the poor quality of their (so-called) MDMA pills forced a massive crash in their market value. In the mid-to-late 80s, a pill would cost as much as $40–$45 (£20–£23), but by 2006, the average street price for MDMA had dropped to around $4–$6 (£2–£3); in fact, some reports put the price as low as 25 cents (15p). Of course, whether there was in fact any MDMA at all in these pills is itself highly debatable. This entire downward spiral in quality ultimately caused older clubbers to give up on pills and turn to the (allegedly purer) "MDMA powder," which looks like cocaine or speed. Prices for this in 2006 were in the region of $60–$100 (£30–£50)—ironically, ten times more expensive than the alleged "Ecstasy." Younger clubbers turned from their older siblings' drug of choice and started using ketamine (an animal tranquilizer) and tragically, most recently, the highly destructive "crystal meth" (methamphetamine).

LOCATION: Pills frequently changed hands between dealers and clubbers alike, making it difficult to pinpoint the origin of manufacture. The first recorded location, where the pill was bought/given/found/acquired, is given here.

TESTED: Various laboratory tests have been carried out; more recently, there have been on-site testing services at clubs as well as the introduction of home testing kits.

LOCATION: NEW YORK, NY
TESTED: 01.11.2000
THE NUMBER RELATES TO SUPERSPY JAMES BOND'S CODENAME, AND IS THE EPITOME OF COOL. THIS PILL WAS AVAILABLE IN NUMEROUS COLORS INCLUDING WHITE, RED, AND GREEN.

007

LOCATION: LOS ANGELES, CA
TESTED: 03.03.2007
THIS BIZARRE DESIGN IS COLD AND CLINICAL, AND WITH ITS OWN TWIST ON THE SMILEY FACE DESIGN— A SYMBOL OF THE ACID HOUSE GENERATION.

45

LOCATION: NEW YORK, NY
TESTED: 08.19.2005
THIS WAS AN EARLY, AND POPULAR, DESIGN THAT REFLECTED LEO ZEFF'S NICKNAME FOR ECSTASY. NOTE HOW IT ALMOST LOOKS LIKE A STANDARD PRESCRIPTION DRUG.

ADAM

LOCATION: FORT LAUDERDALE, FL
TESTED: 08.26.2006
THERE ARE SEVERAL DIFFERENT PLANE DESIGNS AND COLORS ON THESE PILLS. THE MOTIF HAS BEEN USED SINCE 2001—THE INFERENCE PRESUMABLY BEING THAT THE USER'S MIND "TAKES OFF."

AIRPLANE

LOCATION: OSLO, NORWAY
TESTED: 02.25.2005
THE LACOSTE ALLIGATOR, LOGO OF THE POPULAR FRENCH FASHION LABEL, IS RATHER POORLY IMPRINTED ON THIS TABLET.

ALLIGATOR

LOCATION: LOS ANGELES, CA
TESTED: 06.30.2006
BASED ON APPLE MACINTOSH'S FAMOUS LOGO, APPLES USED TO BE VERY POPULAR PILLS, BUT FELL OUT OF FAVOR WHEN THE QUALITY DIMINISHED.

APPLE

LOCATION: MIAMI, FL
TESTED: 06.10.2005
FASHION DESIGNER LABELS ARE ALWAYS POPULAR, SO GIORGIO ARMANI SITS WITH PILLS SPORTING CHANEL, DIOR, AND DOLCE & GABBANA LOGOS.

ARMANI

LOCATION: SACRAMENTO, CA
TESTED: 03.04.2007
THIS DESIGN IS LIFTED FROM THE FAMOUS BAT FROM THE BACARDI RUM BOTTLE. THIS MAY ALSO BE A REFERENCE TO THE COMIC BOOK CHARACTER BATMAN.

BAT

BAPE

LOCATION: SAN DIEGO, CA
TESTED: 03.14.2007
THIS LOGO IS TAKEN FROM TRENDY STREETWEAR
DESIGNERS BATHING APE OR BAPE.

BATMAN

LOCATION: UTAH
TESTED: 11.19.2004
BOTH THIS AND DC COMICS' OTHER CLASSIC ICON,
SUPERMAN, APPEAR FREQUENTLY ON PILLS ACROSS
THE GLOBE.

BEAR

LOCATION: FREMONT, CA
TESTED: 06.30.2006
THE BEAR IS THE STATE SYMBOL OF CALIFORNIA SO
IT'S UNSURPRISING THAT A BLUE VERSION OF THIS
PILL WAS CIRCULATING FREMONT A YEAR EARLIER.

BUDDHA

LOCATION: WEST PALM BEACH, FL
TESTED: 12.01.1999
THERE WERE AT LEAST TWO VARIATIONS OF THE
BUDDHA PILL. THIS ONE IS THE TRADITIONAL CHINESE
VERSION; THE OTHER IS BASED ON THE THAI LOOK.

BUTTERFLY

LOCATION: ONTARIO, CANADA
TESTED: 03.14.2007
BUTTERFLIES, ALONG WITH DOLPHINS AND A VARIETY
OF BIRDS ARE ALL POPULAR CREATURES REPRESENTED
ON ECSTASY PILLS.

CHERRIES

LOCATION: SAN JOSE, CA
DATE: 04.16.2004
THIS LOGO IS THE SAME DESIGN AS THE SUPERCLUB
CHAIN, PACHA, WHICH HAS NIGHTCLUBS AS FAR
AFIELD AS MUNICH AND SAO PAULO.

CLOG

LOCATION: DENVER, CO
TESTED: 08.09.2002
A RATHER UNUSUAL DESIGN HINTING THAT THE PILLS
COME, RIGHTLY OR WRONGLY, FROM AMSTERDAM—
ONE OF THE DRUG CAPITALS OF THE WORLD.

CLOVER

LOCATION: HOUSTON, TX
TESTED: 08.20.2004
THERE ARE MANY VARIED DESIGNS THAT COME
UNDER THE STREET NAME OF "CLOVER"—SEE
"CROSS" FOR ANOTHER EXAMPLE.

CLUB

LOCATION: BOSTON, MA
TESTED: 02.21.2003
THIS DESIGN IS OBVIOUSLY BASED ON PLAYING
CARDS; AND EQUALLY CLEAR CONNOTATIONS
RELATING TO A NIGHT GOING "CLUBBING."

CROSS

LOCATION: CAPE CORAL, FL
TESTED: 04.19.2002
THIS IS AN UNUSUALLY SHAPED PILL, LET DOWN BY
THE BLAND COLOR. A GREEN VERSION OF THIS IS
SOLD AS A "SHAMROCK," OR "CLOVER."

CROWN

LOCATION: SAVANNAH, GA
TESTED: 06.11.2004
THIS DESIGN IS BASED ON THE ROLEX WATCH LOGO,
HINTING AT QUALITY, BUT IN FACT THE PILL ONLY
CONTAINS MDE WITHOUT A TRACE OF ECSTASY.

D&G

LOCATION: SAN FRANCISCO, CA
TESTED: 02.07.2003
BASED ON FASHION DESIGNERS DOLCE & GABBANA.
OTHER POPULAR DESIGNER PILL LABELS INCLUDE
VERSACE AND LOUIS VUITTON.

DAGGER

LOCATION: DALLAS, TX
TESTED: 05.03.2007
THIS GRIM-LOOKING PILL ACTUALLY CONTAINED MORE METHAMPHETAMINE (A.K.A. CRYSTAL METH) THAN MDMA.

DIAMOND

LOCATION: MONTREAL, CANADA
TESTED: 04.07.2006
THIS UNUSUAL BLUE DIAMOND DOES CONTAIN SOME MDMA, BUT IS MOSTLY DIPHENHYDRAMINE, AN ANTIHISTAMINE. IT MIGHT NOT GET YOU HIGH BUT WILL STOP YOUR HAY FEVER!

DOLPHIN

LOCATION: OAKLAND, CA
TESTED: 07.29.2005
COLORS, AS WELL AS DESIGNS, VARY WIDELY BUT ARE NOT REGARDED AS ANY INDICATION OF PURITY ON THEIR OWN. FOR EXAMPLE, DOLPHINS ALSO COME IN A LIGHTER BLUE AND WHITE.

DONALD DUCK

LOCATION: ORLANDO, FL
TESTED: 10.26.2001
THIS RATHER DISCONCERTED/WASTED DISNEY CHARACTER WAS A GENUINE MDMA PILL.

DOVE

LOCATION: SEATTLE, WA
TESTED: 08.09.2002
IN THE MID-90s DOVES WERE HIGHLY PRIZED IN BRITAIN FOR THEIR PURITY LEVEL. SADLY, BY THE TIME THE DESIGN REACHED THE US THAT PURITY HAD WANED—THIS IS A PILL CONTAINING MDA.

DUCK

LOCATION: SAN FRANCISCO, CA
TESTED: 04.04.2003
THIS CUTE DESIGN IS REMINISCENT OF THE SQUIRREL PILL AND MAY BE FROM THE SAME WEST COAST ECSTASY MANUFACTURER.

DUREX

LOCATION: LONDON, ENGLAND
TESTED: 09.23.2003
THIS IS A POPULAR BRAND OF BRITISH CONDOM, SIMILAR TO TROJAN, AND IS OBVIOUSLY A REMINDER TO HAVE SAFE SEX WHEN FEELING "LOVED UP."

EURO

LOCATION: DALLAS, TX
TESTED: 08.19.2005
A RATHER BIZARRE LOGO OF THE EUROPEAN CURRENCY, THE EURO—ALSO A CAPITAL "E" OF COURSE. THIS MAY HAVE BEEN INTENDED TO GIVE THE IMPRESSION TO THE US MARKET THAT EUROPEAN E IS STRONGER THAN THE HOMEMADE PILLS.

EXCLAMATION POINT

LOCATION: LOS ANGELES, CA
TESTED: 08.25.2006
THIS SUPERIOR LOGO IS ORIGINAL AND WELL DESIGNED, A RARITY FOR PILLS. THIS "WARNING SIGN" ALSO GIVES THE IMPRESSION, RIGHTLY OR WRONGLY, OF PURITY AND STRENGTH.

FERRARI

LOCATION: ANN ARBOR, MI
TESTED: 12.02.2005
THE FAMOUS PRANCING HORSE LOGO FROM THE CLASSIC ITALIAN SPORTS CAR MANUFACTURER GAVE THE PILL A FALSE SENSE OF STATUS AND SECURITY. MANY FAMILIAR BRANDS ARE USED IN THIS WAY TO PERSUADE THE CLUBBER TO BUY.

FISH

LOCATION: LOS ANGELES, CA
TESTED: 02.25.2005
GENERALLY A GOOD INDICATOR OF QUALITY, BETWEEN 2000 AND 2005 THE MAJORITY OF PILLS BEARING THE FISH LOGO WERE PURE MDMA.

FLAME

LOCATION: AUSTIN, TX
TESTED: 07.29.2005
THIS RATHER WEAK "FLAMING TORCH" DESIGN IS ALMOST AN AFTERTHOUGHT AND NOT VERY INSPIRING. THE PILL'S PURITY IS NOT KNOWN.

FOXY LADY

LOCATION: BROOKLYN, NY
TESTED: 06.11.2004
THIS DESIGN IS BASED ON THAT OF THE ITALIAN
FASHION LABEL, KAPPA. THE PILL IS A MIXTURE OF
MDA AND MDE, AND NOT THE GREATEST EXAMPLE
FROM THE PERIOD.

GREEN STAR

LOCATION: LOS ANGELES, CA
TESTED: 09.12.2003
THE STAR IS A POPULAR MOTIF ON MANY PILLS AND
COMES IN A VARIETY OF COLORS. WHEN TESTED,
THIS EXAMPLE CONTAINED SIGNIFICANT AMOUNTS
OF MDMA.

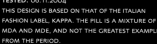

HARRY POTTER

LOCATION: MIAMI, FL
TESTED: 11.15.2002
THE HUGELY POPULAR MOVIES AND BOOKS INSPIRED
ONE MANUFACTURER TO IMPRINT THE FAMOUS
WIZARD'S LOGO ON ITS PILLS.

HEART 1

LOCATION: TORONTO, CANADA
TESTED: 08.28.2006
THIS PILL IS A COMBINATION OF MDA, CAFFEINE,
AND CRYSTAL METH, ALTHOUGH YELLOW VERSIONS
HAVE BEEN SPOTTED IN THE US WITHOUT THE LAST
INGREDIENT.

HEART 2

LOCATION: ATLANTA, GA
TESTED: 03.20.2006
THIS DESIGN IMPLIES USERS WILL GET THAT "LOVED-
UP" FEELING SO MANY LOOK FOR. THE PURPLE HEART,
ALSO A US MILITARY DECORATION, IS ONE OF THE
MOST FAMOUS ECSTASY DESIGNS.

HERS

LOCATION: BOSTON, MA
TESTED: 03.16.1999
THIS DEPICTION OF THE ROMAN GOD VENUS IS THE
UNIVERSAL SYMBOL FOR WOMEN. THIS PILL WOULD
PROBABLY HAVE BEEN MANUFACTURED AS A SET
WITH THE ROMAN GOD MARS—THE MALE SYMBOL—
IMPRINTED ON THE OTHER PILL.

HONDA

LOCATION: HALF MOON BAY, CA
TESTED: 09.10.2004
THIS PILL, IMPRINTED WITH THE LOGO OF THE
JAPANESE AUTO MANUFACTURER, HONDA, WAS
SURPRISINGLY POPULAR.

HORSE SHOE

LOCATION: BUFFALO, NY
TESTED: 04.01.2000
THIS LUCKY SYMBOL OBVIOUSLY HAS POSITIVE
CONNOTATIONS, WHICH HELPED ITS SALES. RARELY
WOULD YOU FIND A PILL IMPRINTED WITH A
NEGATIVE IMAGE SUCH AS A SKULL.

JULIUS

LOCATION: LOS ANGELES, CA
TESTED: 11.04.2004
THIS DESIGN IS THE CLASSIC JULIUS THE MONKEY,
WHICH ADORNS MANY ITEMS IN THE CLOTHING LINE
OF FASHION DESIGNER AND CALIFORNIA RESIDENT
PAUL FRANK.

K PILL

LOCATION: SAN DIEGO, CA
TESTED: 05.13.2005
THE ORIGINS AND SIGNIFICANCE OF THE LARGE K
ON THIS PILL ARE NOT KNOWN. WHEN TESTED IT
CONTAINED NO KETAMINE.

LEXUS

LOCATION: HAMILTON, NJ
TESTED: 06.10.2003
BASED ON THE LOGO OF THE LUXURY AUTO BRAND,
THIS PILL IS ACTUALLY PURE CAFFEINE.

LOVE

LOCATION: MIAMI, FL
TESTED: 10.16.2003
AN UNUSUAL SHAPE AND TEXT COMBINATION MAKES
THIS PILL STAND OUT FROM THE CROWD.

MAPLE LEAF

LOCATION: TAMPA, FL
TESTED: 12.10.2004
AS ITS NAME INDICATES, THE MAPLE LEAF PILL
PROBABLY ORIGINATED IN CANADA, AND MADE ITS
WAY SOUTH TO THE US.

MARTIAN

LOCATION: ARLINGTON, TX
TESTED: 03.21.2003
THIS NON-DESCRIPT ALIEN CARTOON IS THE TYPE OF
DESIGN THAT HAS DRAWN CRITICISM, SUPPOSEDLY
FOR MAKING ECSTASY APPEALING TO CHILDREN. A
SIMILAR ARGUMENT WAS LEVELED AT LSD BLOTTER
SHEETS IN THE 60s.

MCDONALD

LOCATION: SAN FRANCISCO, CA
TESTED: 07.12.2002
PLAYING ON ONE OF THE NICKNAMES FOR E PILLS—
"DISCO BURGERS"— THIS EXAMPLE REPLICATES THE
LOGO OF MCDONALD'S RESTAURANTS.

MEDUSA

LOCATION: SAN FRANCISCO, CA
TESTED: 08.15.2003
THE DESIGN CAUSED THIS BRAND ALSO TO BE
KNOWN SIMPLY AS "WOMAN."

MERCEDES

LOCATION: MIAMI, FL
DATE: 07.27.2003
THE MERCEDES SYMBOL WAS ONE OF THE MOST
POPULAR PILL LOGOS, AND MANY VARIATIONS WERE
CREATED. THIS IS ONE OF THE BETTER DESIGNS.

MERCEDES

LOCATION: SAN FRANCISCO, CA
TESTED: 04.16.2004
ANOTHER ATTEMPT TO TRADE OFF THE QUALITY OF
THE MERCEDES BRAND—BUT THIS IS A POOR COPY OF
THE MANUFACTURER'S LOGO.

MICHELIN MAN

LOCATION: CHICAGO, IL
TESTED: 08.01.2000
BY USING THE LOGO OF THE FAMOUS TIRE COMPANY,
THE MAKERS HOPED TO IMPLY BY ASSOCIATION THAT
THIS WAS A QUALITY PRODUCT.

MICKEY MOUSE

LOCATION: SAN FRANCISCO, CA
TESTED: 08.15.2003
THE FAMILIAR OUTLINE OF DISNEY'S MAIN STAR IS
JUST ONE OF MANY CARTOON CHARACTERS, INCLUDING
BART SIMPSON, TO APPEAR ON ECSTASY PILLS.

MITSUBISHI

LOCATION: NEW YORK, NY
TESTED: 04.22.2005
A DESIGN BASED ON THE JAPANESE AUTO
MANUFACTURER'S LOGO.

MOLLY

LOCATION: LOS ANGELES, CA
TESTED: 03.03.2007
A RARELY SPOTTED CAPSULE CONTAINING PURE
MDMA POWDER. ADDITIONAL MATERIAL IS USED IN
MOST PILLS TO ACT AS A BONDING AGENT—PURE
POWDER DOES NOT BIND WELL.

MONKEY

LOCATION: SAN JOSE, CA
TESTED: 02.24.2005
DESIGN OF A DANCING MONKEY—SO GOOD THAT IT
WAS MOST LIKELY STOLEN, GIVEN THAT VERY FEW
PILLS FEATURED ORIGINAL DESIGNS OF ANY QUALITY.

MOTOROLA

LOCATION: PHOENIX, AZ
TESTED: 07.29.2005
VARIANTS OF THE CELLPHONE COMPANY'S LOGO
HAVE APPEARED ON PILLS WORLDWIDE; THE HIGHLY
POPULAR LOGO HAS ALSO BEEN USED ON MANY
PILLS OF DIFFERENT COLORS.

MTV

LOCATION: LOS ANGELES, CA
DATE: 04.16.2004
BASED ON THE FAMOUS CABLE TV CHANNEL LOGO, THERE WERE BETTER-DESIGNED VERSIONS OF THIS PILL IN CIRCULATION.

NEMO

LOCATION: MEMPHIS, TN
TESTED: 05.04.2004
INSPIRED BY THE 2003 DISNEY MOVIE *FINDING NEMO*, THE FISH EMBOSSED INTO THE PILL DOES NOT LOOK LIKE THE MOVIE CHARACTER IT IS NAMED FOR.

NIKE

LOCATION: CHICAGO, IL
TESTED: 04.03.2002
SOME PILLS' ATTEMPTS TO CASH IN ON RECOGNIZED BRANDS WERE POORLY DRAWN, WITH LITTLE ARTISTIC SKILL OR EFFORT PUT INTO THE PILL MOLD. THIS ATTEMPT AT SPORTSWEAR GIANT NIKE'S FAMOUS "TICK" IS A GOOD EXAMPLE OF BAD EXECUTION.

NUMBER ONE

LOCATION: ORLANDO, FL
TESTED: 04.21.2001
THE INFERENCE MIGHT BE THAT THIS PILL IS BETTER THAN THE REST, BUT IT IS ACTUALLY A POOR-QUALITY MDA PILL WITH A BADLY DRAWN DESIGN.

OMEGA

LOCATION: ORLANDO, FL
TESTED: 08.09.2002
AS OMEGA IS THE 24TH, AND LAST, LETTER OF THE GREEK ALPHABET, THE DESIGN ON THIS MDA PILL HINTS AT THE ULTIMATE END OF THINGS—NOT A GREAT ADVERTISING CHOICE BY THE MAKERS!

PEACE

LOCATION: WEST PALM BEACH, FL
TESTED: 01.10.2003
AGAIN, A NOSTALGIC MOTIF HARKING BACK TO THE HIPPIES' FIRST SUMMER OF LOVE WITH THE CLASSIC PEACE GESTURE. THIS HINTS THAT ECSTASY USERS MAY BE OLDER THAN PREVIOUSLY SUGGESTED.

PENTAGRAM

LOCATION: NEW YORK, NY
TESTED: 06.30.2006
THE PENTAGRAM SYMBOL HAS HAD MAGICAL ASSOCIATIONS THROUGHOUT HISTORY—FOR BOTH PAGANS AND CHRISTIANS. TODAY IT IS USED (IN DIFFERENT FORMS) AS A SYMBOL OF FAITH BOTH BY WICCANS AND PARTICULAR SATANIC CULTS.

PIGGY

LOCATION: LOS ANGELES, CA
TESTED: 10.04.2006
THIS CUTE PILL DIFFERS FROM MOST IN THAT THE DESIGN IS RAISED UP FROM THE SURFACE RATHER THAN BEING EMBOSSED INTO THE PILL.

PINK PIKACHU

LOCATION: ERIE, PA
TESTED: 09.02.2001
THIS DESIGN IS BASED ON A CHARACTER FROM THE ANIME TV SHOW, *POKÉMON*. THE SUPERMAN LOGO IS ANOTHER POPULAR DESIGN.

PLAYBOY

LOCATION: METAIRIE, LA
TESTED: 08.20.2004
THE PLAYBOY BUNNY LOGO WAS A DESIGN THAT CIRCUMNAVIGATED THE GLOBE; EXAMPLES FIRST APPEARED IN BRITAIN AS EARLY AS 1996.

PUMA

LOCATION: SEATTLE, WA
TESTED: 07.29.2005
BASED ON THE LOGO OF THE SPORTSWEAR MANUFACTURER, PUMA; OTHER POPULAR PILL DESIGNS WERE INSPIRED BY THE NIKE AND ADIDAS LOGOS.

QUESTION

LOCATION: ORLANDO, FL
TESTED: 09.10.2004
THERE'S ALWAYS A QUESTION HANGING OVER THE CONTENTS OF A PILL UNTIL TESTED. IN THIS CASE, THE ANSWER WAS 4 PARTS MDMA AND 1 PART MDE.

R

LOCATION: CLEVELAND, OH
TESTED: 03.14.2007
THE R STANDS FOR "ROUGH" AS THIS IS A MIX OF
CAFFEINE, PROCAINE (A PAINKILLER), KETAMINE,
AND A HINT OF MDMA.

RHINO

LOCATION: LOS ANGELES, CA
TESTED: 09.30.2005
THIS UNUSUALLY SHAPED PILL CONTAINS NOTHING
BUT MDA, CAFFEINE, AND FENTANYL.

SAFE SEX

LOCATION: OSLO, NORWAY
TESTED: 06.05.2003
THIS MORE BLATANT SCANDINAVIAN SOCIAL MESSAGE
WARNS OF THE DANGERS OF INCREASED CASUAL SEX
WHILE ON MDMA.

SCORPION

LOCATION: LOS ANGELES, CA
TESTED: 11.18.2005
THIS DESIGN IS DIFFERENT IN THAT IT SHUNS THE
HAPPY, SMILEY VIBE FOR A DARKER, SCARIER LOGO,
ALMOST WARNING OFF, OR PERHAPS DARING, USERS.

SEA HORSE

LOCATION: LOS ANGELES, CA
TESTED: 07.29.2005
THE VARIETY OF DESIGNS, SUCH AS THE SEA HORSE,
AVAILABLE IN LOS ANGELES IN THE EARLY 2000s IS A
GOOD INDICATION OF THE SCALE OF ECSTASY
PRODUCTION AND SMUGGLING IN THE US.

SPADE

LOCATION: SOUTH BEACH, FL
TESTED: 06.30.2006
ANOTHER DESIGN BASED ON PLAYING CARDS, THE
ABUNDANCE OF WHICH PERHAPS SUGGESTS A
GREATER SIGNIFICANCE. CERTAINLY, ECSTASY USERS
ARE "GAMBLING" EVERY TIME THEY DROP A PILL.

SQUIRREL

LOCATION: LOS ANGELES, CA
TESTED: 12.02.2005
THIS DESIGN IS UNCOMMONLY INTRICATE FOR A PILL
AND IS ALSO MADE UP OF REMARKABLY PURE MDMA.

STAR

LOCATION: LAS VEGAS, NV
TESTED: 10.05.2002
LOVELY AS THIS STAR SHAPE IS, THIS PILL CONTAINS
NO MDMA, ONLY DXM—AS WITH MOST OTHER PILLS
BEARING THIS DESIGN.

STICKMAN

LOCATION: CAPE CORAL, FL
TESTED: 12.30.2005
DRINKING A BOTTLE OF BENDRYL ANTIHISTAMINE AND
20 CUPS OF STRONG COFFEE WOULD HAVE ABOUT
THE SAME EFFECT AS THIS PILL. I.E., VERY LITTLE.

SUPERMAN

LOCATION: HOUSTON, TX
TESTED: 05.08.2001
THE SUPERMAN LOGO CAME IN VARIOUS COLORS,
INCLUDING BLUE AND WHITE, AND EVEN AS A
TRIANGULAR SHAPE IN PARTS OF BRITAIN
THROUGHOUT 2001.

TELLYTUBBY

LOCATION: ATLANTA, GA
TESTED: 03.10.2002
BASED ON THE POPULAR CHILDREN'S TV SHOW OF
THE SAME NAME, THIS IS THE CHARACTER PO; THERE
IS A GREEN PILL THAT FEATURES DIPSY.

TOYOTA

LOCATION: ALISTON, MA
TESTED: 08.25.2006
WHEN TESTED, THIS AUTO LOGO PILL CONTAINED
A COCKTAIL OF MDMA, CAFFEINE, PROCAINE, AND
CRYSTAL METH.

TREE

LOCATION: LOS ANGELES, CA
TESTED: 02.25.2005
THIS CHRISTMAS TREE DESIGN WAS PROBABLY LEFT OVER FROM A BATCH CREATED FOR THE HOLIDAY PERIOD, AS SEASONAL DESIGNS ARE NOT UNKNOWN.

TULIP

LOCATION: HOUSTON, TX
TESTED: 05.08.2001
THE DESIGN OF THIS PILL INDICATES IT ORIGINATED IN HOLLAND, SPECIFICALLY AMSTERDAM. THE TULIP IS ALSO THE NAME OF A FAMOUS CANNABIS JOINT.

UNICORN

LOCATION: HOUSTON, TX
TESTED: 05.03.2007
THIS MYTHOLOGICAL BEAST DEPICTED HERE SUGGESTS A FANTASTIC JOURNEY, BUT THE MAIN INGREDIENT IS CAFFEINE.

V8

LOCATION: HOUSTON, TX
TESTED: 03.07.2003
V8 COULD REFER TO EITHER THE POWERFUL CAR ENGINE OR THE HEALTHY VEGETABLE DRINK; BOTH HAVE POSITIVE CONNOTATIONS FOR CLUBBERS.

VW

LOCATION: WEST PALM BEACH, FL
TESTED: 10.05.2002
WHILE CAR LOGOS ARE COMMON DESIGNS, THE VOLKSWAGEN IS ONE OF THE LEAST POPULAR. THIS IS POSSIBLY A NOSTALGIA TRIP HARKING BACK TO THE EARLY 80s WHEN BEASTIE BOY FANS WOULD TEAR THE SYMBOL OFF CARS AND HANG THEM AROUND THEIR NECKS.

WAVES

LOCATION: PHOENIX, AZ
TESTED: 07.01.2005
SOME MANUFACTURERS LACK THE IMAGINATION OR WILL TO CREATE AN INTERESTING DESIGN AND SIMPLY LEAVE THE PILLS PLAIN, WITH A SINGLE SCORE, OR IN THIS CASE, A BASIC PATTERN.

WINE GLASS

LOCATION: LAS VEGAS, NV
TESTED: 08.19.2005
CERTAINLY MORE POTENT THAN A GLASS OF WINE, THE PILL WAS PACKED WITH MDMA, DXM, AND METHAMPHETAMINE.

WOODY WOODPECKER

LOCATION: DENVER, CO
TESTED: 07.09.2002
THIS CHARACTER IS BASED ON THE FAMOUS WALTER LANTZ CARTOONS.

X-FILES

LOCATION: BOSTON, MA
TESTED: 10.05.2002
THE NAME REFERS TO THE CULT US TV SERIES OF THE TIME THAT EXPLORED FRINGE SCIENCE AND CONSPIRACY THEORIES AND HAD ENDED EARLIER THAT YEAR.

X-MEN

LOCATION: LOWELL, MA
DATE: 07.01.2001
THIS IS NAMED AFTER THE MARVEL COMICS' SUPERHERO TEAM WHO OBVIOUSLY HAVE A SHARED MONIKER WITH MDMA'S US STREET NAME, X.

YIN/YANG

LOCATION: WEST PALM BEACH, FL
TESTED: 11.26.2004
THIS PILL, BEARING THE CHINESE PHILOSOPHY SYMBOL, IMPLIES THAT THE USER WILL FEEL AT ONE WITH THE UNIVERSE.

TECHNO, TECHNO, TECHNO

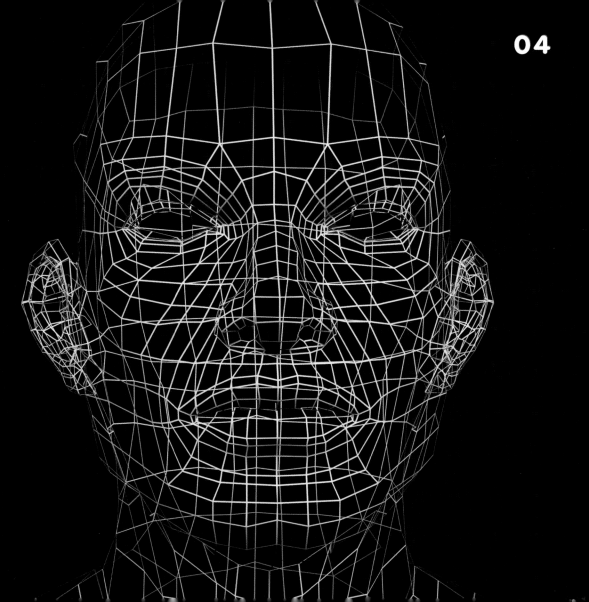

04

04. Techno, techno, techno

Ecstasy is all very well and good when taken in a therapeutic setting, as the early psychiatric pioneers did in the late 70s and early 80s, but why do so many people take it in a club? Apart from its obvious benefit—promoting sociability—the real reason could be down to the music. In 2006, Dr. Michelangelo Iannone of the Institute of Neurological Science in Catanzaro, Italy, discovered that rats given low doses of Ecstasy and then exposed to loud music (95 decibels) experienced increased electrical brain activity. Not only that, but the music made the effects of E last up to five days longer on these raving rodents. While animal experimentation with MDMA is fraught with inaccuracies, it's possible that the same effect is had in humans. It would certainly explain why repetitive beats and loud music have become so entwined with Ecstasy use. But how did dance music develop and become the anthem for the "Ecstasy Generation"?

If you were young, gay, hip, or all three, New York City in the 70s was where it was at.

OPPOSITE LEFT: GAY RIGHTS ACTIVISTS IN NEW YORK IN 1979.
OPPOSITE, RIGHT: GERMAN ELECTRONIC MUSIC PIONEERS, KRAFTWERK, INSPIRED A WHOLE GENERATION OF US DJS AND MUSICIANS.
BELOW: *PADLOCK* LP (1985) FEATURING SLY AND ROBBIE WITH SPECIAL MIXES BY WHEELS OF STEEL LEGEND, LARRY LEVAN.
FOLLOWING PAGES: LARRY LEVAN IN THE DJ BOOTH AT THE PARADISE GARAGE, NEW YORK CITY, IN 1986 (LEFT). THE PHOTO ON THE RIGHT, MADE BY TINA PAUL, SHOWS PEOPLE TRYING TO GET INTO THE LAST FRIDAY NIGHT PARTY ON A SATURDAY MORNING IN 1987. THE CLUB OPENED IN 1976, AND CLOSED ON SEPTEMBER 26, 1987.

New York and Beyond:
The rise of Ecstasy on the dance floor

If you were young, gay, hip, or all three, New York City in the 70s was where it was at. Having demanded—and got—recognition following the legendary Stonewall riots (these involved violent clashes between gays and police at the Stonewall Inn, a Greenwich Village bar, in 1969), the homosexual population was enjoying a hedonistic upsurge in openly gay nightclubs. The euphoric sense of liberation was fueled by Ecstasy, and clubs such as Salvation in Hell's Kitchen were packed to the rafters with young, semi-naked, writhing bodies, shaking their booties to hi-energy dance music and disco.

The introduction of the 12" single in 1975 allowed DJs to mix longer tracks, creating new vibes out on the dance floor; experimental tunes such as Donna Summer's "I Feel Love" and Kraftwerk's *Trans Europe Express* album were pushing the boundaries further still. The increased use of computers and synthesizers in this music was revolutionary. Disco was being transformed into something else, and the man performing alchemy on the wheels of steel was Lawrence Philpot, better known as legendary DJ Larry Levan. Larry was black and homosexual and got his start in gay clubs such as the Gallery and the Continental Baths in Chicago, before moving to New York and the illustrious residency that made his name.

Levan held court at the Paradise Garage every weekend from late 1977 (although the venue didn't officially open its doors until January 1978) until it closed in 1987, and was unafraid to experiment with his audience, playing everything from rock and reggae to European electro and gospel, determined to keep the dance floor buzzing. His skills soon brought him a cult following and fellow DJ innovator François Kevorkian credited Levan with introducing the dub aesthetic into dance music.

When the Garage finally closed, after 11 Dionysian years, Levan couldn't handle it and went on a self-destructive drug binge. He still managed to guest DJ with Frankie Knuckles in the opening weeks of London's Ministry of Sound nightclub, and he toured Japan, with Kevorkian, in the summer of 1992. But ultimately, Levan's coke-and-heroin-driven lifestyle caught up with him and he died in November of that year, of heart failure, aged just 38.

Put your hands up for Detroit!

While Levan was blending a unique sound in the New York clubs, the hometown of another great musical movement—Motown—was giving birth to techno. In the mid-1980s, Detroit was a seething bed of analog synthesizers and early drum machines, such as the Roland TR-909. For a city made famous by mass auto production, machine-made music was entirely appropriate.

The pioneers who blazed the electronica trail of early Detroit techno—Juan Atkins, Kevin Saunderson, and Derrick May—were known as the "Belleville Three." These high-school friends from the Detroit suburbs would soon find their basement-made tracks in dance-floor demand, thanks in part to seminal Detroit radio personality The Electrifying Mojo. Mojo not only played the early homegrown techno tracks, but also influenced the new sound by playing electronic music from techno and electronic music pioneers such as Germany's Kraftwerk, Philip Glass, Manchester's New Order, and Afrika Bambaataa, just as Levan was.

Detroiters traded the choir-friendly vocals of the "house" music coming out of Chicago with metallic clicks, robotic voices, and repetitive hooks reminiscent of an auto assembly line. Many of the early techno tracks had futuristic or robotic themes, although one notable exception was the classic club theme by Derrick May, under his pseudonym Rhythim is Rhythim: "Strings of Life." This floor-filling anthem was packed with rich synthetic string arrangements and took the underground music scene by storm in May 1987 (remixed two years later, it subsequently became an anthem).

OPPOSITE: DETROIT DJ KEVIN SAUNDERSON, ONE THIRD OF THE SO-CALLED "BELLEVILLE THREE," PLAYS HIS HOMETOWN. ABOVE, TOP: DERRICK MAY, A.K.A. RHYTHIM IS RHYTHIM'S FLOOR-FILLING CLASSIC TRACK, "STRINGS OF LIFE." ABOVE, BELOW: "MOVE YOUR BODY" BY MARSHALL JEFFERSON. NEAR RIGHT: JUAN ATKINS IS STILL DJ'ING AFTER 20 YEARS. FAR RIGHT: DERRICK MAY MIXES IT UP FOR A LOUD CROWD.

Techno created a newfound, integrated club scene in Detroit that hadn't been seen in the city since before the Motown label had abandoned Detroit for Los Angeles. The Detroiters had a music to call their own once more. The Belleville Three lived outside the city limits, yet the influence and magnetism of their music—played in loft apartment parties, after-hours and high-school clubs, and on late-night radio—united the listeners of progressive dance music from above and below Eight Mile Road. Techno-friendly regular hours clubs such as The Shelter, The Music Institute, and The Majestic were the hotbeds for progressing the techno movement from basements and late-night radio stations onto the dance floors of the world.

Chicago

Meanwhile—250 miles away—Detroit's musical twin city, Chicago, was developing its own unique dance sound. At the forefront of this movement was a 22-year-old DJ from the Bronx: Frankie Knuckles. Invited to play to the—in his own words—"predominately black, predominately gay" crowd at a new club, the Warehouse, Knuckles started off playing classic gay disco anthems, but then swiftly began experimenting with the records. He would re-edit them on reel-to-reel tapes, creating loops and breaks to raise the dance-floor vibe in new and unique ways. By 1984, he'd started using a basic beatbox and a Roland TR-909 drum machine he'd bought off Derrick May and was playing at a new club, the Powerplant.

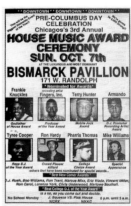

Legendary Chicago radio station WBMX started its own dance-mix radio show featuring seminal DJs The Hot Mix 5: Farley "Jackmaster" Funk, Kenny "Jammin'" Jason, Ralphi "Rockin'" Rosario, Scott "Smokin'" Silz, and Micky "Mixin'" Oliver. All imitated Knuckles and began mixing 12" club singles in an innovative way.

In the meantime, Knuckles' main rival, Ron Hardy, was expressing himself through the tunes he spun at the Music Box, across town. Raw emotion poured out of the speakers getting the crowds hot 'n' sweaty and that energy was distilled into the new music being released by Chicago's new independent record labels DJ International and Trax.

The fast-growing music movement—named after the Warehouse, the club where it all began, with Knuckles—was quickly spreading across the city. At the

OPPOSITE, TOP: A FLYER FOR A RON HARDY GIG.
OPPOSITE, BOTTOM: A POSTER PROMOTING THE
THIRD CHICAGO HOUSE MUSIC AWARDS.
RIGHT, TOP: CHICAGO-BASED DJ FRANKIE
KNUCKLES (HIS REAL NAME).
RIGHT, BOTTOM: RON HARDY, KNUCKLES' PEER,
WITH FRIEND IN 1987.

The drug fed the music, and the music fed the drug in an ever-increasing spiral of mental and communal bliss.

Music Box, the sounds were inextricably becoming entwined with drug culture. Unable to sell alcohol because of licensing restrictions, the Music Box was rife with PCP (angel dust), joints, and the ever-present Ecstasy. The drug fed the music, and the music fed the drug in an ever-increasing spiral of mental and communal bliss. And it felt like it would last forever.

Hi-energy + electronica + Ecstasy = techno x house = acid house

Producers in both Chicago and Detroit used the same hardware and even collaborated on projects and remixes together, and clubs in both cities included Detroit techno and Chicago house tracks in their playlists as club-goers lapped up the cross-pollination. This musical melange blended with Ecstasy in the brain to create a heady brew that was to become known as "acid house." The origin of the term appears to have been lost in the mists of people's brains. Some claim that it was prompted by the fact that people put LSD in the water at the Music Box. Others argue that it was because the music was like a simulated trip, or that it reminded them of acid rock from the 60s. Whatever the reason, the name was to stay for good.

The key to the sound of acid house was a magical little box known as the 303. The Roland TB-303 Bass Line, to give it its full title, was a synthesizer with built-in sequencer made between 1982 and 1983 by Roland, the company behind the already popular 808 and 909 drum machines. The TB-303 (Transistor Bass) was originally made as a bass accompaniment for guitarists when practicing alone. Only 10,000 units were ever made. In the mid-to-late 80s, DJs Marshall Jefferson and Nathaniel Jones (a.k.a. DJ Pierre) were playing around with a 303 in Chicago and produced a track they later

OPPOSITE, LEFT: THE LEGENDARY RADIO DJ TEAM OF THE "HOT MIX FIVE" INCLUDING: FARLEY FUNK, KENNY JASON, RALPHI ROSARIO, SCOTT SILZ, AND MICKY OLIVER.
OPPOSITE, RIGHT: *THE* PLACE TO BE ON A SATURDAY NIGHT IN CHICAGO, THE IRREPRESSIBLE MUSIC BOX.
RIGHT: THE ESSENTIAL TOOL OF ANY DECENT ACID HOUSE REMIXER, THE ROLAND TB-303.

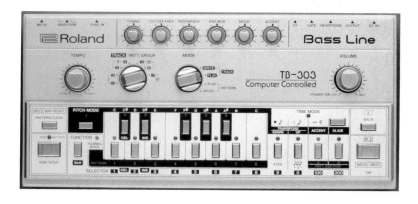

released under the name Phuture: "Acid Tracks." It provided the seminal sound of acid house.

The subsequent demand for 303s was so great that many small synthesizer companies began to produce their own TB-303 hardware clones. In order to cash in on the popularity of the machine, Roland, the original TB-303 manufacturer, eventually released its own TB-303 "clone" in 1996, called the MC-303 Groovebox. The design was flawed, though, and lacked the charisma of the original.

There was something about the sound that the 303 made that fed into a brain under the influence of Ecstasy. It brought the highs, lows, breaks, and builds into a crystal clarity that bound the dancing masses into one huge seething, breathing, dancing organism. Fatboy Slim even paid homage to this marvel of mechanical music with his club anthem "Everybody Needs a 303," a Top Forty hit in Britain in 1997. The defining sound of the movement had been found. The snowball was rolling downhill fast and would soon become an avalanche of new music.

Religious Ecstasy heads for Europe

The music of choice was house and techno, and the drug of choice was MDMA. But the choosers and users of Ecstasy were an eclectic bunch. Initially it was the psychologists and new-age therapists who were made aware of it by Sasha Shulgin and Leo Zeff. Then the clubbers of Texas, New York, Detroit, and Chicago caught wind of the fun to be had. But a more esoteric, spiritual movement soon discovered that "ecstasy" could take many forms—and not just of the religious sort.

For example, Bhagwan Shree Rajneesh (better known now as Osho)—a US-based Indian guru who had developed a strong following since the 60s—was one leader who recognized the drug's uses. Flying in the face of established spiritual leaders, such as Gandhi, the late Rajneesh was quite comfortable with growing material (as well as spiritual) wealth, owning as he did a fleet of Rolls-Royces, several nightclubs, casinos, and publishing companies.

OPPOSITE: POP ARTIST, KEITH HARING, WAS A FREQUENT VISITOR TO NEW YORK'S PARADISE GARAGE NIGHTCLUB AND EVEN DECORATED THE INTERIORS. RIGHT: THE BHAGWAN SHREE RAJNEESH (A.K.A. OSHO)'S FOLLOWERS WERE PARTLY RESPONSIBLE FOR THE INFLUX OF ECSTASY FROM THE US BACK TO EUROPE.

"I just remember that there were 300 people there, the two dealers had 1,300 Es and they completely ran out and had to go and get more."

DJ David Holmes, recalling a 1991 rave in a Northern Irish castle

"The only time I took Ecstasy was years and years ago. It was absolutely amazing."

Graham Norton

His ranch in Oregon had a no-drugs policy but several followers who were former therapists had already been switched on to the curative powers of MDMA, and were soon using it in all sorts of ways. "The euphoric mood-altering drug Ecstasy was discreetly slipped into rich sannyains' drinks just before fund-raising interviews," wrote Rajneesh's former bodyguard, Hugh Milne in his exposé, *Bhagwan: The God That Failed*.

As the drug's usefulness spread among the disciples, networks of distribution were set up across the US, and then throughout the rest of the world, in the early to mid-80s. According to Arno Adelaars' 1991 book, *Ecstasy*, "The Dutch followers of Bhagwan were taking so much Ecstasy that several supply lines were necessary to meet demand."

This—coupled with all the roadies, producers, musicians, and DJs hopping back and forth across the Atlantic with orders for more and more E for the clubs of England, Ibiza, Belgium, and Holland—meant that after 70 years of "exile" in the US, MDMA was returning home to Europe in style.

The French scene

In Europe, things were also picking up, but in a different way. House music had hit continental Europe with the rise of acid house, rave, techno, and funny-shaped pills in the late 1980s. Frenchman Laurent Garnier was working in the French Embassy in London before he was drawn northward to the nascent rave scene in Manchester, where people were downing Ecstasy like there was no tomorrow. He soon became one of the prime movers in the late 80s "Madchester" scene. Garnier's DJ'ing at the Haçienda club provided the inspiration for bands such as The Stone Roses and Happy Mondays to begin adding house rhythms to rock music to create the "baggy" sound, and—like all good DJs—Garnier span the musical spectrum from classic deep house and Detroit techno, to hard acid/trance and jazzy tracks. "Ecstasy made the whole thing happen," recalled Garnier. "It was a completely black dance-orientated thing in the beginning, especially in Manchester, and then Ecstasy brought all the white people in. I think it just turned the world upside down completely."

Simultaneously, in France, an 18-year-old, Bob Sinclar (a.k.a. Christophe Le Friant) started DJ'ing in 1986, specializing in funk and hip-hop music, under the pseudonym of Chris The French Kiss. His first club hit was "Gym Tonic," a collaboration with Thomas Bangalter of Daft Punk, which sampled a Jane Fonda workout tape. Sinclar popularized the "French touch" of house music, with heavily sampled and filtered disco strings. In 2001, he created the Africanism project, via which a mix of DJs and musicians—including another important French DJ, David Guetta—produced house music with a combination of Latin, jazz, and African tribal flavors.

Garnier eventually headed back to his home country to do his national service in the early 90s—in time to catch the rising surf of French dance music. He ran the Wake Up club in Paris for three years before recording his first LP, *Shot in the Dark*, in 1995. This was followed by a second, *30*, in 1997, which included one of Garnier's best-selling singles, "Crispy Bacon." After trotting the globe on extended DJ tours throughout the late 90s, Garnier returned to the studio to record *Unreasonable Behaviour*, which was released in early 2000.

OPPOSITE, TOP: FLYER (FRONT AND BACK) FOR A FRENCH RAVE, PYRAMID.
OPPOSITE, BOTTOM: AN INVITATION TO MANCHESTER CLUB THE HACIENDA'S FIFTH BIRTHDAY PARTY, IN 1987.
BELOW: FORMER HACIENDA DJ, PRODUCER, AND RECORDING ARTIST, LAURENT GARNIER.
BELOW, RIGHT: FRENCH TECHNO DUO, DAFT PUNK, IN THEIR PERENNIAL DISGUISES.

Garnier, Sinclar, and Guetta were leading lights for French dance music and helped shape its evolution, but French house was also greatly influenced by the late 70s "space disco" sounds—the likes of Sarah Brightman singing "I Lost my Heart to a Starship Trooper," Sheila B. Devotion's "Spacer," and the P-funk music of George Clinton and Bootsy Collins. Those artistic influences and sci-fi themes became an essential part of the movement, and French electronica bands took up the mantle—witness the hugely successful and danceable Daft Punk, with their sub-Kraftwerk robotic personas. The Parisian duo of Thomas Bangalter and Guy-Manuel de Homem-Christo formed an electronic double act in 1993 and achieved massive global success with their 1997 album *Homework*. They were clearly influenced by the Detroit and Chicago sounds, as Bangalter confirmed in a 1997 *Mixmag* interview: "Before us you had Frankie Knuckles or Juan Atkins and so on. The least you can do is pay respect to those who are not known and who have influenced people." But interestingly, the duo was not as into the drugs as Garnier. "Personally I don't like Ecstasy," stated Bangalter. "It makes me lose any sense of critical judgment—it makes me like every track I hear. All the music we've done, I think people can enjoy it and really go crazy even if they're not on any drugs. Maybe that's why it's successful and has crossed over."

At the same time that Daft Punk were making sound waves, other French bands, such as Cassius and Stardust, were creating their own floor-fillers and there was a constant cross-pollination of the bands' influences on each other. The sophisticated Gallic groovers had made their mark all over the continent. But not far away, another offshoot of dance music was being nurtured . . .

Belgian hardcore

Elsewhere in Europe, a new sound was developing, driven by the gay dance scene. "Eurodance," as it became known, was a fusion of house, rap, and hi-energy disco. The combination featured much faster bpms and the strong use of female vocals, often mixed with a male rap solo. Tracks like "Strike It Up" by Black Box (1990) and "Rhythm is a Dancer" by Snap! (1992) had the stylings of a eurodance duet, and "Everybody's Free (To Feel Good)" by Rozalla (1991) had the characteristic synthesizer riff. Other hit singles included famous anthems like "It's My Life" (1992) by Dr. Alban and "What Is Love" (1993) by Haddaway.

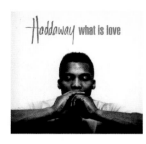

By the late 80s and early 90s, eurodance and house music had become synonymous with Belgium and the Netherlands, via the emergence of Belgian "new beat." The Belgian scene was primarily centered in and around the small town of Ghent where such clubs as The Number One, Tiffany's, and The Twenty-seven packed in dancers every weekend, but the daddy of these clubs was Boccaccio Life. Robert De Maesschalck, the owner of Boccaccio, originally founded Balmoral in 1963 in the town of Destelbergen, near Ghent, as a dance and party hall. Nine years later, in 1972, De Maesschalck opened the diamond-shaped Boccaccio, and it was soon outshining its older sibling. The club became the hot bed for Belgian new (or euro) beat, and fans flooded in from across Europe. The "Bocca"—as it was affectionately known—played electronic body music (EBM) at very slow speeds, in contrast to other eurodance tracks. (Legend has it that one of the DJs, possibly Olivier Pieters or Henk, played an EBM record at 33rpm instead of 45rpm and new beat was born.) Popular groups that took off included Lords of Acid—whose explicit lyrics and samples, "Darling, come here / fuck me up the . . .," and sexually themed acid house tracks caused a sensation. However, like so many nightclubs of the era, The Bocca was forced to close after a long series of drug problems. As the music and Ecstasy were so intrinsically linked, it was practically impossible for many club owners to separate the two, particularly when the criminal gangs who started managing the security, were also selling E inside the venues. Very often, the police's sledgehammer approach was simply to revoke the club owner's license. But Belgium and the Netherlands "remain the most important Ecstasy source countries," according to the United Nations 2005 World Drug report. When asked, 23 percent of countries named Belgium as the main source of Ecstasy exports while 28 percent of the world's MDMA seizures happened in Holland in 2003.

Speaking of which . . .

Holland

While across the rest of Europe the American style of house was gaining more widespread acceptance—with Belgian band Technotronic's "Pump Up the Jam" (1989), along with Snap's "The Power" (1990) topping the charts—in Holland it was an entirely different matter. Predominately more liberal toward alternative lifestyles than its EU partners, the Netherlands soon became the epitome of "faster, harder, louder, more!" when it came to dance music and drugs. (Ecstasy wouldn't become illegal here until 1988.) A new, faster (over 180bpm—as opposed to the usual 120bpm) version of techno developed, called "gabber." "When you go to a gabber club, what moves in your body? It's your head," enthused Laurent Garnier, with a head-banging motion, to *Mixmag* in 1997.

The commercial version of gabber—happy hardcore—topped the music charts across Europe, and as far as dance bands go, they didn't get any more commercial than 2 Unlimited. The band formed in 1991 when two Belgian producers—Phil Wilde and Jean-Paul de Coster—decided to cash in on the European techno/eurodance/house explosion by hiring Dutch duo, rapper Ray Slijngaard and singer Anita Doth. Wilde and de Coster had created an instrumental track called "Get Ready For This" but decided that it needed some vocals, so they asked Slijngaard to rap on it. The track was licensed in Britain by legendary producer Pete Waterman, who removed all the vocals except for the

28 percent of the world's MDMA seizures happened in Holland in 2003.

line "y'all ready for this?," sampled from The D.O.C.'s "It's Funky Enough." The single was an instant hit, reaching No.2 in the UK charts. Over the next five years, the act sold an incredible 18 million records globally. 2 Unlimited's mind-numbingly repetitive "No Limit" was released in January 1993 and became their most successful single ever, reaching No.1 in 12 European countries. Regardless of the phenomenal success, however, they were criticized heavily and the press dubbed them "2 Untalented." UK weekly pop bible *Melody Maker* carped that they were "juvenile" and "puerile," but conceded "2 Unlimited stand for energy and excitement." The band's manager, Michel Maartens, felt that 2 Unlimited's

LEFT: THE FIRST SUMMER OF LOVE IN 1967 SET THE STANDARD FOR THE NEXT GENERATION, 20 YEARS LATER. HOWEVER, WHILE THE ORIGINAL HIPPIES WERE CHILLED OUT ON MARIJUANA AND TRIPPED OUT ON ACID, THEIR CHILDREN PARTIED MUCH HARDER TO FAR MORE URGENT MUSIC.

success was that they were launched at a time when, "Many parents feared that house and techno would damage their children. It was associated with pills and nightly escapades. But Ray and Anita proved to be the acceptable faces of techno. When Mum and Dad saw they were harmless pop stars, all mistrust was over."

Of course, parental approval was exactly what the kids didn't want. By April 1996, 2 Unlimited's flame had died and the band split. Wilde and de Coster tried to recapture the magic with another Dutch singing duo, but failed to rekindle the public's passion. 2 Unlimited had finally discovered their limit.

The Second Summer of Love

In 1967, a seemingly limitless mass of hippies were flocking to San Francisco—many wearing flowers in their hair, as ordered by Scott McKenzie's famous song—as a generation was switching on to LSD. It was a gradual process that culminated, mid-year, in "The Summer of Love." During "Human Be-in" events in Golden Gate Park, as many as 100,000 "flower children" descended on the city. The mass exodus westward and the cultural upheavals the drug brought slowly spread across the world, and very soon kids from all over Europe were heading off in search of enlightenment, fun, and good drugs to the far-flung corners of the world on the so-called "hippie trail." One of the first stops on the road that would invariably lead to Marrakech and Katmandu was a small Spanish island in the Balearics called Ibiza.

Many hippies never got any further than this Mediterranean paradise and soon a small commune began to blossom there. Clubs like Amnesia and Pacha opened in the early 70s and rapidly evolved from primitive hippie hangouts to fully fledged superclubs, to rival New York's Studio 54 and the Paradise Garage, as disco fever gripped the island. Stars such as Grace Jones, Freddie Mercury, and Bryan Ferry jetted in to enjoy the champagne-and-"Charlie" lifestyle in the opulent clubs. House music and Ecstasy also jumped on a plane and crossed the Atlantic to set the Iberian nightlife alight, but the drug's use was still fairly limited to an in-the-know elite.

As the island partied into the early 80s, a new breed of tourist invaded Ibiza: the British working-class lad and ladette, as the media would later label them. Many of these "scallys," "dodgy geezers," and n'er do wells spent the summer committing small robberies in order to fund their partying lifestyle. They started going to Pacha, and Ecstasy became the catalyst for democratizing the club scene in Ibiza. It broke barriers—suddenly, regular working-class people could literally rub shoulders with the stars, and everyone was cool about it.

In September 1987, a now-legendary posse went out to the island in the sun to celebrate DJ Paul Oakenfold's birthday. With him were DJs Johnnie Walker and Danny Rampling and smooth-talking entrepreneur Nicky Holloway. Their well-documented Ecstasy epiphany changed the course of music in Britain forever. "It was almost like a religious experience," Walker recalled. "A combination of taking Ecstasy and going to a warm, open-air club full of

"Pacha encapsulates both the spirit of Ibiza and the spirit of disco, that is why it is unique."

Simon Dunmore, Defected party night organizer

beautiful people—you're on holiday, you feel great and you're suddenly being exposed to entirely different music to what you were used to in London. This strange mixture was completely fresh and new to us, and very inspiring." So inspiring that, after a week of wandering around San Antonio out of their heads and wearing moonboots, they had resolved to evangelize the music and the drug back in England. At the forefront was Rampling who, with his then girlfriend Jenni, staged a party in a fitness center in south London two months later. The night was called Shoom and it would prove to be one of the most important catalysts for dance music in the UK.

And so, from the seeds sown 20 years earlier, the children of the "flower children" were about to discover their own Summer of Love. For 1988 was the year Britain went "mental."

"I don't know if you know how important the Paradise Garage is, at least for me and the tribe of people who have shared many a collective spiritual experience there. The Garage also changed or affected my life incredibly through various 're-imprinting' experiences and transformations."

Keith Haring, *Pop Artist*

"It's a massive problem and it's come upon them almost without warning. What we're encountering are literally hundreds of cases a month of psychotic, bizarre reactions from people who've been using ecstasy."

White House drug czar Barry McCaffrey, August 1, 2000

Serotonin stories:
Better living through chemistry

When a Canadian female student went to a wedding rave, little did she realize it would be a life-changing event. She later recounted her experience on Nicholas Saunders' Ecstasy.org:

"Myself and friends were invited to a wedding on a small island off the coast of Vancouver Island. The wedding was that afternoon on some bluffs overlooking the blue, calm waters of the Pacific. It was truly beautiful. Our excitement for the after-wedding rave mounted. The wedding couple arrived with some Es and we each had one capsule. I felt nothing for some time. The amazing thing is you sit there and wait, and then suddenly, without knowing it, you have entered a blissful state.

"My first indication that I was rushing was that the beat of the bass from the techno began to fill my brain and I was unable to sit still any longer. I reached the middle of the dance floor and let the music take me to heights I never dreamed imaginable. I lost all self-consciousness, and felt in tune with the music, as though the bass was a life force and I was connected to it. My movements became fluid and I was able to dance along with it in utter freedom and abandon. Everyone else was on their own trip, yet I felt connected to them because we were all experiencing the same amazing feelings.

"A feeling of utter and sheer joy shot through my body making me vibrate and glow with warmth and energy. It was as if at that moment I understood what love really is, I felt as though I understood so many more things than ever before, the mysteries of life opened up to me. I must have spent the next several hours dancing, time lost all meaning. I looked around me and everyone was lost enjoying the truly ecstatic feeling that this amazing drug brings. Everyone around me was caring and warm. If anyone bumped into anyone, we would say sorry and then sometimes hug. People shared lollipops with each other. At one point I was dehydrated and a girl I didn't even know went and got me a bottle of water. I was amazed at how unselfish everyone was.

"I suddenly felt like I knew exactly who I was and what I wanted out of life. I reached a state of amazing clarity and purity."

"I felt love that night, and I saw that human beings could be wonderful and beautiful. Before, I had been feeling untrusting and frustrated by people, but now my outlook had completely changed. Everyone smiled and hugged each other. I felt that life was something wonderful and precious, that life was something so much more than I had ever understood. I suddenly felt like I knew exactly who I was and what I wanted out of life. I reached a state of amazing clarity and purity. I felt all inhibitions and boundaries fall away from me. Everyone there seemed like a beautiful person, inside and out. I felt like no one was judging anyone, everyone and everything was accepted.

"One thing Gary said stuck with me, 'Last night was the closest I ever came to feeling part of a tribe.' I felt as though we had become a close-knit family. I now know that this weekend has changed my life. It's not just the E, I feel like I have really learned something from all of this. It is hard to put into words. Basically, I feel more in touch with my feelings and myself. I know where I am heading in life. Life seems like a wonderfully exciting adventure to me now, just full of experiences waiting to happen. LIFE!!! It's something to be tasted, something to be lived to the fullest. I wonder if people live their lives and never reach this kind of spiritual understanding. I feel like a new person, I feel like a joyful person, and I want to share this joy with others. I hope that what I have described can maybe help others learn too . . ."

MAD FER IT!

05. Mad fer it!

In the winter of 1987, things were looking bleak in Britain. Margaret Thatcher and the repressive Conservative Party were well into their third term of office. The wild, carefree summer in Ibiza seemed very, very far away and the post-rave, post-vacation blues were kicking in for all those Brits returning to a cold, wet, gray country. "That was a rather depressing, down-tempo time. It was the start of the British recession and there wasn't a lot to offer young people in England," DJ Alex Gold remembered. But Danny Rampling was not a man to be downhearted. He had a mission to spread the word of MDMA and rave music, and he threw himself into his newfound destiny with all the passion of a zealot.

Shoom

"Ibiza changed my life . . . That first visit [in 1983] had me hooked," enthused Rampling, years later. Once back in England he and his future wife, Jenni, desperately looked around for a venue from where they could preach the good word from behind their twin-deck "pulpits." Their gospels were the 12 inches of vinyl: house music. Their sacrament: MDMA. Finding a venue to kickstart a cultural revolution proved difficult, and the revolution started rather ignominiously, in a gym—the Fitness Centre—in Southwark, south London. On a cold November night they opened the doors to the club that would be known as Shoom, the name signifying the rushing feeling of coming up on E. That night, Rampling and Carl Cox DJ'ed to an eclectic mix of some 70 house and funk fans. "It was a shaky start," recalled Rampling, "but it was fun, hence the enthusiasm to do it again."

Word began to spread. The Ramplings handed out free Lucozade and Perrier water, and clubbers were encouraged to express themselves as creatively as possible. People started turning up in fancy dress, gave out candy, and acted like big kids, and by January the Shoom "family" had adopted the archetypal 70s smiley face as its emblem; the logo that would be splashed everywhere over the course of the next decade, expressing the "Happy, happy, happy" vibe. Shoom moved to the YMCA on Tottenham Court Road in

"[Although Shoom was just] a smoked-filled room filled with an outrageous mix of people, I feel we shifted a paradigm within youth culture and music. Shoom created music opportunities for everyone who was involved. It felt like we were having the time of our lives, really."

Danny Rampling

London's West End as the loved-up crowd continued to grow. As word got around about this unique club experience the lines outside grew and grew. Jenni Rampling soon gained a reputation as the most ruthless door operator in London, and before long the celebs turned up wanting a piece of the action. Initially they were refused entry, but soon the likes of Boy George, Patsy Kensit, and ABC's Martin Fry were getting preferential treatment over the original Shoom members. It all turned sour in 1989 as the newspapers started to vilify ravers. "The press didn't like the acid house movement and were out to use people as scapegoats," Danny recalled in *DJ* magazine in 2007. Rather than face a media witch-hunt, he shut down Shoom, the club that helped launch acid house culture virtually overnight, while simultaneously providing a basis for mass Ecstasy use in Britain.

Rampling continued his career in music as a DJ and producer, remixing many British and international acts. He joined the BBC in 1994 and presented the Lovegroove Dance Party on Radio 1 for an impressive eight years, finally laying down his vinyl and retiring from full-time DJ'ing at the end of 2005, to concentrate on running a restaurant. "I've always had a real passion for food," he explained at the time. "Now, instead of creating layers of music, my skills will be converted to layers of flavors—not on a turntable but on a plate."

Heaven's future

While Rampling was running Shoom, fellow Ibizan convertee Paul Oakenfold was planning his own Balearic-inspired night, with visionary pals Ian St. Paul and Trevor Fung in Streatham, London. They called it the Project, after their favorite bar in Ibiza. The after-hours club opened illegally from 2am till 6am as lost revelers snuck in the back door and found a little slice of the Mediterranean isle to dance away in. Unfortunately, the police caught whiff of what was going on, raided the club and shut it down.

Not to be defeated, the dynamic dance duo of St. Paul and "Oakey" (as Oakenfold was affectionately called) moved their night to a small back room in the renowned gay nightclub Heaven, underneath London's Charing Cross railroad station. Their Future night was a shoestring affair, as they couldn't afford door staff. It soon became popular, however, and the two realized that they needed a bigger venue. Goaded on by Ian St. Paul, Oakenfold carried out the unprecedented act of setting up a club night in the 1,500-capacity main room of Heaven on a Monday. People called them fools. Their first night, on April 11, 1988, and now renamed Spectrum, saw 100 people through the door.

FUTURE FUTURE

THE ORIGINAL AND ONLY BALEARIC CLUB DANCE YOU FUCKERS!

DJs PAUL OAKENFOLD
TONY WILSON

HUNGERFORD LANE
OFF CRAVEN ST.

£5.   10–3.30am

EVERY THURSDAY

MANAGEMENT RESERVE THE RIGHT TO REFUSE ADMISSION.

The next two weeks yielded only a small increase in numbers. Oakenfold and St. Paul were soon £12,000 in debt to Richard Branson's club and were becoming concerned, but they kept faith in what they were doing. That faith was rewarded on the fourth week, when they had a staggering 1,200 mentalists through the door looking for a "bangin'" time. The club had reached its tipping point and was never less than full after that. The curtain had been well and truly raised on Spectrum's "Theatre of Madness."

The Trip

The third piece of the acid house clubbing puzzle was completed by Nicky Holloway. The DJ was Rampling's mentor and, spurred on by his friends' successes at Shoom and Spectrum, he was inspired to set up his own club: "We all felt that this thing was growing," Holloway recalled in 2007. "I thought, 'Well if they can fill a big place playing this music, then maybe I can, too.'"

Four months later, on Saturday, June 4, 1988, Holloway launched his first Trip party at the Astoria in London's West End. It marked the point at which the underground dance culture became a high-profile, full-fledged mass-movement. Many early clubbers blamed Holloway for "ruining" the scene, but with hindsight it was inevitable. Thousands of blue-collar ravers descended on the Astoria and Ecstasy use became rife, with dealers blatantly offering MDMA even beneath the "No Drugs" policy signs. Britain's archaic licensing laws were still in place, meaning that when the Astoria had to shut at 3am, all the punters still up for clubbing spilled out on to the streets, shutting the roads and dancing on cars in scenes reminiscent of something out of the movie *Fame*. When the confused police turned on their sirens to disperse the crowds, the clubbers simply cheered and danced to the noise, yelling "Can you feel it?"—the lyrics to Todd Terry's "Can You Party?," which featured a loud siren.

But The Trip, Spectrum, and Shoom weren't the only happening clubs. There was RIP, Hedonism, The Underground in Liverpool, The Garage in Nottingham, Frenzy in Brighton, Slam in Glasgow, and of course the Haçienda in Manchester. The cultural explosion was happening across the country and it was about to get even larger and messier as it spilled out of the clubs and into Britain's green and pleasant fields.

The Great Outdoors

If Danny Rampling was the golden child of acid house, then Tony Colston-Hayter became its whipping boy. Having had his eyes opened at Shoom, Colston-Hayter—a successful schoolboy entrepreneur—saw there was money to be made in rave. He was seen by the original Ibiza hardcore as brash and arrogant and was soon exiled from Shoom, but when he saw the scale of Spectrum and The Trip he was motivated to start his own event, Apocalypse Now, at Wembley Studios in August 1988. He had an open policy cutting across the class and racial divides, but his flash persona brought him trouble. In September, the media were starting to take notice of the burgeoning rave culture, and unlike Rampling, Holloway, and Oakenfold, Colston-Hayter stuck his head above the parapet and appeared on British TV's News at Ten. It was to open the floodgates for police persecution of the whole scene.

Realizing his mistake, Colston-Hayter renamed his events Sunshine, and when the police shut down his next London rave, he decided to take 1,000 clubbers out to the country. He'd hired an equestrian center in Iver Heath, just outside London, and blew ravers' minds with dry ice, green lasers, and stunning music. As the sun came up, people picked flowers and hugged in the fields in scenes reminiscent of 1967's Summer of Love.

After an event in London's Docklands that the press managed to infiltrate, Colston-Hayter was plastered across the tabloids as the "Acid House King," condemned for running an "evil night of Ecstasy," and accused of luring innocent 15-year-olds into his drug den—all the while making thousands of pounds in profits. It was standard scaremongering by the press, but it was affecting business—and Colston-Hayter himself. "He paid the price for speaking to the press because he had MI6 [Britain's intelligence service] on his tail. He was followed. His phone was tapped. He was harassed. They put him through hell, actually," mused Danny Rampling, ruefully.

But Colston-Hayter refused to be beaten: the raves must go on! And so they did, regularly attracting 4–5,000 "up for it" ravers who were willing to travel miles for the freedom to party and "get on one" all night. By now, Colston-Hayter had made his old friend Dave Roberts a business partner—Roberts dealt with security, trying to prevent gangs from muscling in on the lucrative business.

Clubbers would slowly come down in the warm sunshine of a summer sunrise, more often than not changed by the night's events.

It was a long hot summer in 1989 and the raves seemed like unstoppable behemoths of hedonism rolling across the British countryside. But the dark clouds of repression were gathering overhead.

Twenty thousand people standing in a field

As the rave scene moved out of the cities and into the surrounding green fields, a new form of communication was adopted to notify ravers where to go. Pirate radio stations would broadcast meeting venues (these were often motorway cafes), and then a convoy would be led to the venue. But the police soon picked up on this and simply waited for large groups to gather before promptly shutting down the motorway. Tony Colston-Hayter then discovered British

"My best mate and I decided out of the blue to try some Es and check out this club called Millionaires. We just decided to try it thinking it would be a bit of a buzz. Little did I realize how this one night would change our lives . . . suddenly I was 'There.' At one point I recall clasping my hands over my head 'cos I thought it was going to take off . . ."

Mark Wyss, British clubber from Cheshire

"As soon as people realize that the majority of people in this country take drugs then the better off we'll all be. It's not like a scandalous sensation or anything like that . . . drugs is like getting up and having a cup of tea in the morning."

Noel Gallagher

Telecom's Voice Bank, a new answerphone system with which he could change messages remotely from a cell phone; this meant he could release the address of the event at the very last minute, enabling the 24-hour party people to get to the rave before the police.

The whole illegal rave movement that started around London saw ravers and police playing cat and mouse as they drove all the way round the city's circular highway, the M25—the motorway that inspired the moniker of ambient techno band Orbital. Others also set up massive raves in the country such as Energy and Biology, and all over Britain ex-clubbers were hanging around in lay-bys waiting for the call that would reveal the location of the secret venue.

The whole scene was captured perfectly in Pulp's acerbic single, "Sorted for E's & Wizz," which damned the whole culture in 1995 with the lyrics "Is this the way the future's supposed to feel? Or just 20,000 people standing in a field." And "It's 'Nice one!' 'Geezer!' But that's as far as the conversation went." Ironically, the press completely missed the point (yet again) and attacked lead singer, Jarvis Cocker, for "glorifying" drug use. Admittedly, the single's CD sleeve *did* contain instructions on how to make a paper wallet to hold drugs, which prompted Britain's *Daily Mirror* newspaper to run a front-page story with the headline "Ban This Sick Stunt." The media were in such a frenzy that simply mentioning the word Ecstasy would see celebrities pilloried in the press. "The thing with the tabloids is that they can't deal with ambiguities," Cocker told *Melody Maker* in 1995. "They have to see things in terms of black and white, and that's not what the world's really like." With the press, the police and even the government becoming involved too—questions were now being asked in Parliament—it was all going to end badly, for sure.

The Madchester scene

Before the rave scene exploded across Britain in 1988 and the country's youth embarked on the exciting new adventures of Ecstasy and acid house music, there were still a few pieces of the puzzle to fit. Once in place, these pieces would ensure that dance culture would become a global phenomenon.

When Mancunian Renaissance man and TV presenter Tony Wilson set up his Factory Records label in 1978—after an epiphanic moment seeing the

Sex Pistols perform—he probably had no idea of how it would change the face of British dance music. He signed legendary indie band Joy Division; after the band's lead singer, Ian Curtis, committed suicide they reformed as New Order and started concentrating on electronic music. In 1982, Wilson persuaded members of New Order to become partners in a nightclub he set up called the Haçienda. Initially, the club played guitar-based indie tunes; takings were not good and things were looking bleak. Then along came local DJ Mike Pickering, a Northern Soul survivor who'd had hits in the gay, black nightclubs of the US. Pickering saw that the Haçienda had the potential to become like New York's Paradise Garage, and set to work hiring an up-and-coming band called the Happy Mondays to play their first gig there in 1983. The Mondays' sound was a mix of "Funkadelic, One Nation Under the Groove . . . Northern Soul . . . punk rock . . . Jimi Hendrix . . . Captain Beefheart. And a load of drugs on top of that," explained lead singer Shaun Ryder—a man whose capacity for drug consumption would rival that of The Rolling Stones' Keith Richards.

By November 1984 Pickering and Martin Prendergast were DJ'ing at the Nude club night in the Haçienda, playing electro, hip-hop, funk, and techno-pop. There was something in the air. Two years later the night was legendary, and turned the Haçienda from a loss maker to being full every night of the week. Other Manchester clubs started to follow, including the Boardwalk, Konspiracy, House, Soundgardens, Man Alive, and Bugsy's in Ashton-Under-Lyne.

By 1988, DJ Graham Park had joined Prendergast and Pickering in the Haçienda's booth and another new influence had arrived in town: Ecstasy. This was the drug the Happy Mondays had been waiting for, and they actively set about evangelizing it—helped by the fact that a friend of theirs was bringing the drug into the country from Amsterdam. According to another Haçienda DJ, Dave Haslam, "Ecstasy use changed clubs forever; a night at the Haçienda went from being a great night out, to an intense, life-changing experience."

Apart from lead singer Shaun Ryder, the Happy Mondays' most notorious member was Ryder's school mate, Bez, who leapt around the stage like an epileptic stick insect, waving maracas, while off his face on E. Somewhat implausibly, he was destined to become a modern British folk hero.

Elsewhere in Manchester at the same time, dance acts like 808 State and A Guy Called Gerald were starting up, inspired by the Chicago imports that were being played in the clubs. Other bands from the north-west, such as the Inspiral Carpets, The Stone Roses, and Liverpool's The Farm were now mixing traditional guitar indie sounds with the new ethic of dance music, just as the Mondays were doing, giving rise to what was to become known as the "Madchester" or the "baggy" sound.

But the one thing that saved the Haçienda and started the whole scene—Ecstasy—was also to spark its downfall. As the dealers became more ruthless, and violent, there were several shootings in and outside the club; and as the security problems increased, the police became an oppressive, almost constant presence. Eventually, in June 1997, the Haçienda was shut down, leaving debts of £500,000 ($900,000) and a tragic history of violence no one could have foreseen ten years earlier.

E would also be the Happy Mondays' Achilles' heel. When they started work on their last album in 1990, most of the bandmembers were doing so many drugs that Factory Records sent them to Barbados to record it—the island was supposedly free from Ecstasy. Unfortunately, it was in fact rife with heroin, and the band spent so much money on drugs they ultimately bankrupted their record label. The album, *Yes, Please!*, was released two years late, in October 1992. It earned an acerbic review from the British music magazine, *Melody Maker*: "No, thanks."

Panic on the streets of London . . . press and politics go wild!

As dance culture continued to spread out to a wider audience, the sensationalist tabloid press began to pick up on it. Unfortunately, media-naive organizers like Tony Colston-Hayter and Nicky Holloway, who launched The Trip at the Astoria, set themselves up as targets for the generally hostile press and were vilified as evil drug barons.

In the early days, most of the media had either ignored the druggy overtones to rave culture, or were at least neutral about it. They were confused at first, unsure which way to go. Was this some great new craze for the kids or something more sinister? The press's hypocritical—nay, schizophrenic— approach to acid house was best exemplified by *The Sun* on October 12, 1988, when the paper offered readers the chance to buy a "groovy and cool" acid house T-shirt: "Only £5.50, man." The concept and language showed how out of touch the media were, but that didn't stop them wanting to make money out of the youth movement.

But suddenly something changed in November 1988, when *The Sun* began running big scare stories, such as "Evil of Ecstasy: Danger drug is sweeping discos and ruining lives," or the more moderate, "Shoot these Evil Acid House Barons." They even withdrew their T-shirt offer, with the explanation, "Sadly, events have tarnished acid house's reputation. We detest the drugs on the fringes of this scene." Various music stars like Boy George and DJ Mark Moore were wheeled out to "Say No to Drugs."

The tabloid press became insistent that acid house parties were a threat to the British nation, peddling fanciful stories about pernicious drug pushers manipulating vulnerable young ravers. The most outrageous lie was *The Sun*'s report that following one rave, "Beheaded pigeons littered the floor of the hanger after Sunday's party. Youngsters were so high on Ecstasy and cannabis they ripped the birds' heads off."

In October 1989, Kent police formed the Acid House Squad specifically to stop rave parties through mass arrests. The following year saw the government allow extended licenses for certain nightclubs, beyond 3am, a major reason why illegal raves were set up in the first place. One London club, Turnmills, even got to stay open 24 hours a day. This was an attempt by government to turn people back to the controlled environments rather than have them running all over the countryside.

Parliament debated the dangers of acid house and in July 1990, The "Bright Bill" became law. Anyone organizing an illegal rave without a license, or outside

Despite heavy police presences, most rave shut-downs were annoying, but relatively peaceful, events.

OPPOSITE: THE COVER OF *YES, PLEASE*—THE LAST ALBUM TO BE RELEASED BY THE HAPPY MONDAYS BEFORE THE BAND SPLIT UP. **RIGHT**: HAVING SHUT DOWN ANOTHER ILLEGAL RAVE HELD IN THE BRITISH COUNTRYSIDE, THE POLICE CONFISCATE THE DJ'S EQUIPMENT.

licensing hours, would now face a £20,000 [$40,000] fine and/or six months in prison. The police's dilemma was that ravers at these events were happy, they were dancing peacefully, and there was no violence—but raves were now illegal and arrests had to be made.

That was still not enough for the Conservative government, however, and in 1994 they passed The Criminal Justice Act, which removed right to silence, permitted the police to take and retain intimate body samples, and increased the police's "stop and search" powers. The act was specifically aimed at destroying the rave scene.

Police were now allowed to shut down a "gathering on land in the open air of 100 or more persons (whether trespassers or not) at which amplified music is played during the night . . ." Music was defined as "sounds wholly or predominantly characterized by the emission of a succession of repetitive beats." Many pundits pointed out that under the terms of the act, the audience at an amplified classical concert for invited guests on private land could now, in effect, all be arrested too.

Resistance to the act came in the form of the Advance Party, a group made up of an alliance of sound systems and civil liberties groups, and two demos were organized in London on July 24 and October 9, 1994. The latter saw a march that ended up as a party at Hyde Park. But rave music had become too politically hot, and the police were determined to shut it down. When the mounted police charged, the crowd of 5,000 moved toward them; faced by the storm of bottles and sticks thrown at them, the police retreated. But by 10pm, word circulated that all the gates had closed and the crowd were all hungry, tired and it felt like a good time to leave.

OPPOSITE: PROTESTORS AT A DEMONSTRATION AGAINST THE CRIMINAL JUSTICE ACT IN LONDON IN 1994 DEMAND THAT BRITAIN'S CONSERVATIVE GOVERNMENT "KILL THE BILL."
BELOW: ETERNITY, A RAVE MAGAZINE, WAS FIRST PUBLISHED IN 1992 TO KEEP CLUBBERS UP TO DATE WITH NEWS AND EVENTS.

Various dance acts made their own—less violent—protests, such as Orbital's *Are We Here?* EP, which had a mix entitled "Criminal Justice Bill?," consisting of four minutes of silence.

Over time, however, the constant harassment by police, The Criminal Justice Act, threats from drug dealers, and the extended licensing laws saw the rave scene slowly fade away. Organizers had simply had enough—they'd had a good run, but now it was over. Rave came out of the fields and warehouses and back into the clubs. Acid house culture was becoming "legitimized" and commercialized.

CzechTek 2005

But police intervention, intimidation and aggression are sadly not limited to Britain, or even to the dim past. As recently as 2005, Czech ravers discovered to their cost that not everyone was as "loved-up" as themselves and that people who didn't like them were bent on becoming the ultimate party poopers.

The first major rave festival in the country, CzechTek, happened in 1994 at Hostomice with a modest 300 ravers. It was based around the concept of free parties for all, a concept that the infamous Spiral Tribe started in Britain and which then spread to Europe. After the success of 1994, a CzechTek festival was held every July in the Czech Republic—each time at a different location. As a non-commercial festival, it usually took place on ex-military land or in a field. There was little or no organization, and it lacked even the basics of toilets, drinking water, and garbage collection. In true early UK-rave style, the location of the festival was usually only revealed on Czech rave websites a day before the techno festival was due to take place.

Initially a legal event, as the numbers swelled to 10–20,000 CzechTek went rogue. As the event grew, the Czech media began to portray it as a haven for drug abuse; locals in neighboring villages complained about the loud noise, lasting for days, and about the mess left behind. Police were regularly accused of incompetence for not dealing with the problems. All this public pressure culminated in the disastrous events of 2005.

The 5,000 ravers at Mly'nec had no idea what was happening when 1,000 heavily armored riot police tore into them, using tear gas and water cannons. They also brought a tank. The ensuing battle left 37 dancers and 47 police officers injured, and one fatality: a raver who had been run over. The event caused a massive political scandal, and came as something of an uncomfortable reminder of the former communist state's heavy-handed actions 16 years earlier. Protests were set up outside the Czech interior ministry. The Prime Minister, Jirí Paroubek, didn't make the situation any better by stating that the techno fans were "not dancing children, but dangerous people." But the president, Václav Klaus, called the violence "hard to excuse."

Typically, though, after a few weeks the protests and media attention fizzled out, and eventually all charges against the police were dropped. The following year, CzechTek became a legal, officially sanctioned event once more, attracting some 40,000 ravers. It passed off without any major incident.

The 2005 battle highlighted what ravers, travelers, and Ecstasy users across the world are constantly fighting: repressive governments who are unwilling to understand the freedom of expression that the drug and music actively encourage. Ironically, however, this freedom was about to be packaged, bottled and sold back to the masses in a commercial form . . .

"I used to take two Ecstasy pills, break them into quarters, and put them on the corners of the two turntables, and work my way through them as a DJ set went on. I played Donna Summer, Kraftwerk, Public Image Ltd., The Beatles, the Stooges, anything. It really felt like something was happening."

James Murphy, NY DJ and founder of LCD Soundsystem

"Ecstasy is a love drug. There was a TV program about drugs the other day, and even they had to admit that basically Ecstasy killed off football egotism. 'Cause it used to be a real big problem in England: every football match would be mobbed by a huge ton of gang fights. It kind of stopped about a year after Ecstasy came out. They always used to sing, 'You're going to get your fuckin' head kicked in.' And then they started singing, 'Let's all have a disco [biscuit] and go funkin' mental . . ."

Norman Cook, a.k.a. Fatboy Slim, 1999

Serotonin stories:
MegaDogs martial arts!

This British university teacher of organic chemistry had some interesting insights into the nature of Ecstasy and ancient martial arts when he posted this observation on the late Nicholas Saunders' website, Ecstasy.org:

"In 1992, I tried half of a 'Rhubarb and Custard' with my girlfriend and some other friends, now all Doctors of Chemistry like me. Although not very strong, it made me think, 'Hmmm, there's something to this.' Anyway, I entered Megadogs [a club night] full of ravers like myself, and had a few of the best times of my life.

"About this time I started doing tai chi. After about a year I was struck by the remarkable similarity between the 'inner peace and clarity' of the state of mind attained by about an hour of focus on tai chi and 100mg+ of MDMA. In fact, the closest I have ever come to the euphoria I experienced initially on E was by doing tai chi. The combination of E + tai chi was quite amusing, because any focus on my body or breathing in a tai chi way gave me waves of euphoria, regardless of how little or much effort I put into the exercise. Once the initial overwhelming tingles had subsided, I could also understand what my teacher was getting at. It seemed to make me far more sensitive to my own body's energy and enabled me to correct my posture to ensure more effective energy flows. I used to do tai chi and E at raves, and it enhanced the E feelings enormously. I think the sensations enhanced by 4/4 beats and all that can be extended to this idea about focus on breathing and 'internal' rhythms.

"After a couple of years, I found that the honeymoon period was drawing to a close. What was missing? After talking to lots of disenchanted clubbers I came to the conclusion that MDMA feeds on excitement and novelty. After a while, the brain assimilates a lot of experiences, and comes up with an 'ideal' which must be met in order to have a good night: good music, friendly doorstaff, no queues for the toilets, room to dance—yet a feeling that the dance floor is full—and intimate, cool conditions, smiles from strangers, all the

"After about a year I was struck by the remarkable similarity between the 'inner peace and clarity' of the state of mind attained by about an hour of focus on tai chi and 100mg+ of MDMA."

people you are with having an excellent time, free water, interesting light shows etc, etc. Many now only use amphetamines because they get too disappointed compared with the euphoria of their first few times.

"I've now developed some tai chi exercises that I can do without looking too conspicuous at raves, and are quite an acceptable alternative to MDMA. Although tai chi can never recreate the oneness and empathy of initial E experiences, no one has the crushing disappointment that a 'pear-shaped' evening on MDMA can generate.

"MDMA is an astounding discovery. It has helped to change the way I think, and I don't know anybody who hasn't found it fascinating and enlightening. If used intelligently I think it has tremendous potential as a therapeutic tool."

US & WORLD RAVE-O-LUTION

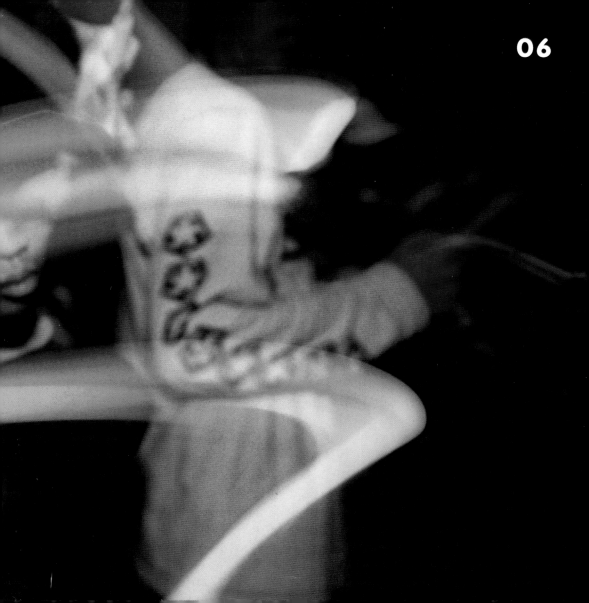

06. US & World Rave-O-lution

Britain's burgeoning rave scene revolutionized that country's youth culture in the 1980s, but it took a little longer for grand-scale parties to take off in the same way in the US. That's not to say that people weren't popping pills and raving in America—but the partying was on a more "intimate" scale, recalling the birth of house and techno in the clubs of New York, Chicago, Detroit, and Houston.

The man credited with being responsible for bringing raves to the US on a large scale was Brooklyn-born Frank Mitchell. Also known as "Frankie Bones," Mitchell was an established New York City DJ, who had visited Britain to check out the rave scene in 1988. He began DJ'ing there too, and when one 1989 rave he attended attracted 25,000 people—five times more than expected—Bones realized something was happening that he had to take back to the US.

On his return to Brooklyn in 1992, Bones duly began staging his Storm Raves. Unlike the British raves he'd experienced, these were small affairs with only 50 to 100 people taking part. Bones projected videos of the British raves on the walls to educate the acid house neophytes, and to liven up the atmosphere, but the blessed-out, loved-up vibe found at the British raves was hard to recreate in the early days—when a fight broke out at one of them, Bones (ironically, in view of his message) screamed over the sound system "If you don't start showing some peace, love, and unity, I'll break your fucking faces." His plea for peace, love, unity, and respect (PLUR), however, was to become the founding principle of good practice across the rapidly growing US rave scene. By December 1992 the Storm Raves were attracting some 5,000 party people to the abandoned warehouses and loading docks of Queens and Brooklyn that Bones selected as his venues.

Bones' Storm Raves also provided the opportunity for many soon-to-be-famous young DJs, from Doc Martin and Sven Vath to Josh Wink, to cut their teeth on the decks. One attendee, Tommy Sunshine, described his first experience at a Storm Rave in Mireille Silcott's *Rave America: New School Dancescapes*: "There was a twenty-five-foot chain-link fence between the crowd and the DJ booth . . . he's playing records, thrashing around like he's in a fucking punk band . . . he smashes the record on the wall behind him. There are kids climbing all the way up the fence—25 feet high, hanging onto the fence, screaming 'Faster! Faster!!!!' and he's playing tracks that are 180 BPMs! These New York maniacs want it faster?! . . . I don't think I could talk for three weeks after I came home. I was shell shocked."

"People liked strict hip-hop—there were no such thing as ravers in 1990 . . . [When] the PLUR thing came about, it was PLUM, actually. Peace, Love, Unity, Movement . . ."

Frankie Bones

West Coast Collectives

Bones, and other DJs, were also spreading the word on the West Coast, and some of the earliest US raves were held in San Francisco. Soon they were being staged in Los Angeles, and elsewhere in California, with various collectives being formed to hold their own raves. One of the key founders of the San Francisco scene, Malachy O'Brien, had first moved to the Bay Area in 1989 from Manchester, England. He worked at a bar, Ten 15 Folsom, where fellow co-workers included many future rave progenitors, such as Preston—who helped start Toon Town, the city's first major mixed-gay-and-straight house club—as well as O'Brien's Come-Unity partners, Simon and Kosmic Jason.

By 1991 the San Francisco house scene was beginning to take off, with parties such as Osmosis at the old DV8, Sundays at Mission Rock, Colossus, Love, and Mr. Floppy's Flop House. O'Brien, who had witnessed the beginnings of rave culture back in Britain, knew that the next logical move was to take the raves outdoors: "I was working at Ten 15, and one night word got out that we would do a party at Baker Beach," O'Brien recalled. "There were only 50 or 60 people that night. The DJ decks were set on a crate, and Jëno [the DJ] had to kneel down in a hole in the sand. It was very renegade."

Soon O'Brien joined forces with the Wicked posse and Martin O'Brien of the Gathering, and set up the Full Moon parties. These full-scale raves—the first of which were held in San Francisco's Candlestick Park—soon became legendary. Also in 1991 O'Brien and Simon launched the Come-Unity parties at Ten 15 Folsom, which Malachy viewed as a communal, peaceful platform for his eco-spiritual views on house music culture. His Come-Unity flyers read, "When used with positive intention, Group energy has the potential to restore the plan of Love in Earth. When you open your heart and trust the whole group you dance with; when you feel love with everyone, and they return it, a higher vibration can be reached. This happens when a crowd is deep into the vibe of house."

Returning from a particularly successful Full Moon beach rave in March 1993, tragedy befell O'Brien. Catching a lift back to San Francisco with some friends he sat in the back with the huge sound system. Pretty soon everyone in the van feel asleep from the exhaustion of dancing all night. Including the driver. The van crashed and the sound system crushed O'Brien's spine, paralyzing him from the neck down.

Yet O'Brien remains positive both about his own future, and about the healing power of rave: "It's hard to disassociate or give up on those ideals. I want to see it come back again strong. Not to be evangelical, but to see the message come through again would be very positive. Those feelings that we had at the time seemed pure; we thought we could change the world."

The Midwest & Florida

Frankie Bones' Storm Raves also inspired two guys from Milwaukee, Kurt Eckes and Patrick Spencer (also known, respectively, as Jethro X, and Jedidiah the Messiah), to set up their own raves in 1992. The Drop Bass Network (DBN), as it came to be called, was a key rallying force in the nascent Midwestern rave scene. DBN staged outdoor weekender events called Even Furthur, as well as more than 70 one-off parties, including spectacular New Year's Eve raves. In comparison to what was happening elsewhere in Chicago and Detroit, DBN was much darker, hardcore and further underground—they referred to themselves as "Techno Pagans" and used satanic imagery in their publicity materials and light shows. As founder Jethro X explained, "We're pagans. We worship big walls of

"I've always accepted drugs like Es and acid as being part of the rave scene, because people took them to get into the music. Now there are all these other drugs, like crystal meth and heroin, that the kids are taking, and drugs like this don't really relate to the music. Now, although I've never thought of this before, I'm thinking that drugs could destroy our scene."

Kurt Eckes (a.k.a. Jethro X)

sound. We believe in decadence and hedonism . . . doing drugs and listening to really heavy music." Drop Bass were key supporters of hardcore techno and gabber with their rallying cry, "Can you pass the acid test?" For over 10 years DBN were the center of Midwestern rave, and DJs and producers such as Speed Freak, Lenny Dee, Delta 9, and Tron, and fellow co-organizers such as Core Innovations, ATP, Mushgroove, Incredibeets, and Mile High ensured that Middle America got to rave as much as the East and West Coasts.

Meanwhile, down in Florida another scene was going strong, spearheaded by the likes of DJ Icey (also known as Eddie Pappa). The Florida-born DJ, who was raised on a diet of early 1980s new wave synth pop, industrial, and hip-hop, began DJ'ing in the early 90s at The Edge in Fort Lauderdale. Proving that nothing exists in a vacuum, he began experimenting with the Big Beat sound that Norman Cook and The Chemical Brothers were playing in Britain, and Icey was the prime founder of Funky Breaks and Florida Breaks. Icey is generally credited with getting "The Chemicals" their first US show, and when British DJ and producer Pete Tong heard an early single produced for Icey's Zone Records label in 1996, he signed the big-beat precursor Galaxy Breaks to his FFRR label.

ART BY KUZICH ● 415/543-2270

Just as DJ Icey was cutting his teeth in the music scene, in March 1985, the first Winter Music Conference (WMC) took place in Miami, set up by Louis Possenti and Bill Kelly. While initially intended as a music industry event for producers, acts, DJs, A&R staff, and record companies to get together and talk business, it has subsequently evolved into a hedonistic dance fest and is now an essential date in the international clubber's calendar. In 2007, a staggering 1,780 acts and DJs entertained a crowd of over 40,000 there.

"This week is like club-music heaven for the fans," commented Rob Fernandez of the New York branch of international superclub chain, Pacha. "It's the only time you can hear every major dance-music act in the world at the same time, and there's nothing else anywhere that rivals this week. Winter Music Conference helps create stars." UK superstar DJ Carl Cox simply described it as "Hot. Excited. Lovable. Dark. Interesting."

"The force that through the green fuse drives the flower drives my red blood; that blasts the roots of trees is my destroyer"

join us at the northern naked end of baker beach on saturday, june 20

potluck at four, weather permitting

fire at sundown

LEFT: THE CLIMAX OF THE BURNING MAN FESTIVAL, WHEN THE 80FT EFFIGY IS TORCHED DURING AN ALL-NIGHT RAVE. **ABOVE:** THE FLYER FOR THE FIRST "OFFICIAL" BURNING MAN FESTIVAL; IT WAS HELD ON BAKER BEACH, SAN FRANCISCO, IN 1986.

Burn that mother down

The rave culture that was springing up around the US was leaking out into alternative scenes, embracing travelers and creative souls who work outside the mainstream. One festival in particular eventually came to embody the ultimate mecca of liberated lifestyles and freedom of expression: the Burning Man, held in the Black Rock Desert in Nevada, 90 miles (150km) north-northeast of Reno, every September. Described by organizers as "an experiment in community, radical self-expression, and radical self-reliance," it takes its name from the ritual of burning a huge wooden sculpture of a man on the festival's sixth day.

The event was inspired by sculptor Mary Grauberger, a friend of co-founder Larry Harvey, who held spontaneous art-party gatherings on Baker Beach, a cove frequented by nudists. Around the summer solstice, Grauberger's parties would culminate in the burning of sculpture. When Grauberger stopped holding her parties, Harvey picked up the torch and ran with it, starting the first Burning Man event in 1986. Harvey, Jerry James, and a few friends met on the beach in San Francisco and burned an 8ft-high (2.4m) wooden man and his small wooden dog. In 1987, the effigy had grown to almost 15ft (4.6m) tall, and by 1988 it had mushroomed to a height of some 40ft (12m). John Law and other members of the prankster group the Cacophony Society got involved in Burning Man the following year, when the police shut down the burn, and instigated a move from Baker Beach to Nevada's Black Rock Desert.

By 2004, the Burning Man was a towering 80ft (24m) high and the festival was attracting 30,000 attendees. As the event has grown, the organizers have been forced to strike a balance between the freedom of participants, the requirements of various land-management agencies, and the police. Over the years, numerous bans on fireworks, firearms, and dogs have been introduced. Some artists and visitors to the earlier Burning Man events believe the underlying freedoms and concepts of the Burning Man event have been reduced or eliminated by these restrictions, leading to criticism of the current event as being too structured and controlled.

Burning Man has developed a reputation for drug use, which is hardly surprising in a place where, as one journalist noted, "every single thing everywhere smells like some combination of sweat and dust and marijuana and urine and fire and tequila and glue." Ritualized Ecstasy use occurs frequently, as Michelle Goldberg reported for *Salon* magazine: "It was drugs, finally, that opened Burning Man up to me. My whole group dropped E for the culminating ritual . . . When it was time to leave, I asked everyone I'd come with whether they would have loved Burning Man if they hadn't been on drugs. No one said anything for a moment, and then Bjorn, one of only two Burning Man veterans among us, said yes, but not nearly as much. Despite what the organizers say— that you don't need drugs because the festival is already an altered reality— many of the attractions would have been incomprehensible sober." The on-site police do come down hard on people they catch taking drugs, though.

I Fought the Law . . .

Statistically, drug use in the US was always slightly lower than in Britain, and experimental Ecstasy use by American teens increased by just 5 percent, from 7 percent to 12 percent, between 1999 and 2001.

Regardless of this, the US government was becoming increasingly concerned about the drug and rising rave culture. The Ecstasy Anti-Proliferation Act of 2000 increased sentences for trafficking 800 MDMA pills by 300 percent, from 15 months to 5 years. It also increased the penalty for trafficking 8,000 pills by nearly 200 percent, from 41 months to 10 years.

In January 2000, the State Palace Theater in New Orleans was the site of a monthly rave that was infiltrated by the bête noire of all fun-lovers, the US Drug Enforcement Agency (DEA). Under the federal "crackhouse law," which makes it a felony to maintain a building for the purpose of drug consumption, the DEA and then US Attorney Eddie Jordan attempted to jail three of the theater's promoters. The Prosecution reasoned that (a) people come to raves; (b) people who come to raves sometimes use drugs; (c) promoters must know this (especially in light of the presence of "drug paraphernalia" such as bottled water and glow sticks); and therefore, (d) a rave must be an event that takes place "for the purpose of drug consumption."

The lengthy trial ended in a plea bargain. Barbecue of New Orleans, Inc., the company that had hosted the party, was fined $100,000, and the judge ordered that "rave toys" be banned from the building. Also, any room kept 15 degrees cooler than the rest of the theater was prohibited—so no chill-out rooms allowed! US attorney Jim Letten called the plea "an immediate, tangible, and long-lasting benefit to the welfare of local youth and the community as a whole." But he was premature in his assessment, as all the charges against the promoters were ultimately dropped and the theater continued to stage raves. Not one genuine drug bust was made and, two months later, another judge ruled that the banning of rave toys violated the First Amendment.

. . . And the law won

The authorities continued to insist that the drugs, not raves, were the enemy, while completely missing the point that the drugs ARE raves—but not necessarily the other way round. As with what had happened in Britain a decade earlier, a repressive government was facing a culture they couldn't

control. As Dr. Julie Holland pointed out, "Drugs are subversive. They make those in power nervous." So the powers-that-be stamped down hard. And the propaganda machine is big and powerful. The DEA misleadingly warns on its website about the dangers of Ecstasy "and other predatory drugs . . . drugs like Ecstasy—that are often advertised and 'tested' as safe, are neither. The tests are unreliable, and Ecstasy is never safe at any dosage level."

The RAVE act saw electronic music groups across the US, such as ROAR, AuraSF and Freedom to Dance, organize protests in Austin, LA, New York, and Seattle—they even held a rave on the manicured turf of Capitol Hill in Washington, D.C.

LEFT: KILLJOY WAS HERE: EXECUTIVE DIRECTOR OF THE UN OFFICE ON DRUGS AND CRIME, ANTONIO MARIA COSTA, BELIEVED DRIVERS SHOULD BE STOPPED AND TESTED IN THE US IF SUSPECTED OF BEING UNDER THE INFLUENCE OF MDMA.

To back up this continued attack on MDMA, the Reducing Americans' Vulnerability to Ecstasy Act—commonly known as the suspiciously named RAVE Act—was proposed in 2002 by Joseph Biden, a Democrat senator from Delaware and pre-eminent crusader in the War on Drugs. The act was intended "to prohibit an individual from knowingly opening, maintaining, managing, controlling, renting, leasing, making available for use, or profiting from any place for the purpose of manufacturing, distributing, or using any controlled substance, and for other purposes." However, it also stated that if certain items such as massage oils, menthol nasal inhalers, and pacifiers, "that are used to combat the involuntary teeth clenching associated with Ecstasy," were found on a site, they should be regarded as "drug paraphernalia" and indicated that the promoter was aware there were drugs on the property.

Dissenting voices argued that now the police could effectively arrest and charge any concert promoters so long as glow sticks and bottled water were present at their venues. Congress was accused of picking an easy target in the public eye to keep up support for the War on Drugs, and that the First Amendment right to freedom of assembly would be violated. Public dissent was powerful enough to have the act shelved.

Although the RAVE Act was not passed, another act—essentially the same in all but name—sneaked through Congress on April 30, 2003, piggybacking on the Amber Alert Act, which was aimed at improving ways of spreading information about abducted children to the general public. The deceitful way the Illicit Drug Anti-Proliferation Act (author, one Senator Joseph Biden) was smuggled through Congress helped avoid any debate, and merely highlighted that it was deeply flawed, like its predecessor.

In 2005, Antonio Maria Costa, the Executive Director of the United Nations Office on Drugs and Crime, advocated drug testing on US highways to help prevent drug use at raves. "The high-octane, psychoactive drugs that make these Raves, or ritualized drug parties, so dangerous fall under our purview. Member States have a special obligation to reduce the harm these events hold for young people. Their drug habits may not become life-long, but the drugs they take, and the behavior these drugs trigger, may well end many lives before they've begun," said an ill-informed Costa.

Ibiza, The Dog's Balearics

Across the waters, however, Ibiza's clubs were under no such threats from the authorities: indeed, they were going from strength to strength. Pacha and Amnesia's transformation from lowly farmhouses, through 70s champagne and coke chic, up to superclub size was making the island THE holiday destination for real party people.

Another club, Ku in San Rafael, a short distance from Amnesia, first began life as a restaurant in the 1970s. Its opulent décor attracted the likes of Freddie Mercury, soul legend James Brown, and Grace Jones. Local DJs such as Alfredo Firorillo, an Argentinean, pioneered Balearic beat in the 1980s—an eclectic mix of electronica, Latin, Afro, and funk flavors. His sets at Amnesia were a key influence on British DJs such as Danny Rampling and Paul Oakenfold, inspiring them to take the music back home and start their own clubs.

In 1989, Pepe Rosello—an Ibiza nightclub owner since 1963—took over an old conference hall/disco and the revolutionary Space opened its doors. Space took clubbing to the extreme and only shut for two hours a day (in line with Spanish licensing laws). Since 1999, it has become the ultimate after-club club, opening at 8am on Sunday and shutting at 6am the following Monday. Early DJs to play there included Britain's Alex P and Brandon Block and it has since seen sets by top names such as Carl Cox, Sasha, Erick Morillo, Sven Vath, and Paul Oakenfold. Space's infamous outdoor terrace is built right next to the airport, giving clubbers the experience of witnessing huge planes constantly roaring overhead, the sound mixing in with the dance beats.

The 1990s were a more profit-driven time on the island, with big-boy promoters Cream, Ministry of Sound, and Manumission arriving to hold special nights for the summer season. The music evolved into house and trance, and admission prices increased. This period also saw the introduction of a host of side attractions at the clubs, including outrageous publicity stunts, live sex shows, and stilt walkers.

In 1994, brothers Mike and Andy McKay arrived on the island, fresh from promoting their Manumission nights in Manchester. They had originally intended to start organizing parties in Morocco, but decided on Ibiza when they realized that flights to the island were cheaper. Over the years, the club

OPPOSITE: THE CROWD ON THE TERRACE AT IBIZA'S SPACE DANCE THE AFTERNOON AWAY AS PLANES SCREAM OVERHEAD ON THEIR APPROACH TO THE AIRPORT. THE CLUB'S ALL-DAY SUNDAY EVENT IS THE PERFECT WAY TO CONTINUE THE EXCESSES OF THE PREVIOUS NIGHT.

night moved venues from Es Paradis to Pacha and finally to Privilege (the renamed Ku)—the world's biggest nightclub, according to Guinness World Records. Manumission's huge, lavish weekly shows cost over $400,000 to stage. And each year things got bigger, better, and madder, until the club and its promoters came to embody the very essence of Ibizan debauchery. Matters reached a peak in 1998 when media coverage of Ibiza went ballistic, and tales of excesses at the Manumission hotel (captured in a banned movie) made Mike and his then girlfriend (now wife) Claire household names; mostly by regularly having sex on stage in front of 10,000 clubbers.

By the time 2006 rolled around, 1.67 million visitors were hitting the island looking for a good time, with just over half a million of them from Britain.

But the island's history of partying reveals that nothing stays the same. "Three years ago we were looking at Ibiza and feeling a bit pessimistic," said Manumission's Andy McKay in 2007. "I just felt there was nothing for the next generation. The DJs were getting older. It was an older clubbing population and no one seemed to care that we had got these 16-years-olds saying, 'It has got nothing to do with my life.'" So the Manumission co-founder set up "Ibiza Rocks," importing the new wave of guitar-based indie bands such as The Fratellis, CSS, and Kasabian in to do live gigs. Clubbing on the island had changed once more.

Cream, Ministry, and the rise of the superclub

Inspired by the huge clubs that were being set up in the Balearics, several promoters started setting up giant "superclubs"—and in turn, clubbing superbrands—back in Britain. Two of the biggest were The Ministry of Sound in London, and Cream in Liverpool.

Liverpool's Merseyside Academy had originally opened as a student

BELOW, LEFT: HUSBAND AND WIFE, MIKE AND CLAIRE FROM MANUMISSION, AFTER HAVING SEX ON STAGE IN FRONT OF 10,000 COMPLETE RAVERS.

BELOW, RIGHT: EXHIBITIONISM, EXPRESSIONISM, AND EXCESSIVENESS WERE THE ORDER OF THE DAY DURING MANUMISSION'S HEYDAY.

OPPOSITE: TODAY, THE CREAM BRAND IS SO WELL-KNOWN IT IS ONLY NECESSARY TO SHOW THE LOGO AND THE TAGLINE "CREAM. IT'S A PART OF YOU"—AND EVERYBODY UNDER THE AGE OF 30 KNOWS EXACTLY WHAT IS BEING PROMOTED.

concert venue, but it was never truly successful, and was bought by Stuart Davenport and Lennie MacMillan, who turned it into a nightclub called Nation. In October 1992, a new night of house music, Cream, was launched there by James Barton—to little fanfare. After three weeks, Davenport and MacMillan were ready to close the Cream night as so few people were turning up, but as with Oakenfold's Spectrum night in London's Heaven, something magical happened: the crowds arrived, and Cream went on to thrive.

Paul Bleasdale was Cream's main resident DJ early on (he finally retired in 2002), while house pioneer Paul Oakenfold filled that post between 1997 and 1999. But the club night also played host to many international DJ superstars, including Sasha, The Chemical Brothers, and Paul van Dyk. Ironically, Cream became so successful that Barton eventually bought Nation from Davenport and MacMillan.

But Cream was destined for greater things than a mere few nights in a Liverpudlian club. Barton was determined to transform it into a global dance brand, and began to market the Cream name aggressively. Today, Cream has its own record label, and runs its Creamfields dance festivals in nations from Russia to Brazil, Argentina to Poland, Chile to the Czech Republic, with attendances of well over 20,000 at each event.

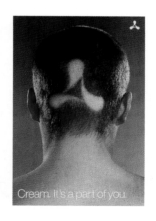

Cream. It's a part of you.

The Ministry of Sound was always designed to be big and corporate. Founded by Humphrey Waterhouse, DJ Justin Berkmann, and James Palumbo, the club opened in the fall of 1991 and filled up by word of mouth in a series of secret gigs, until the "official" opening in 1992.

Straight away the club looked toward maximizing revenue from sponsorship and licensing deals (for everything from stereos to clothing); it also set up its own record label. Palumbo became rich— and he was also completely of the establishment, even helping draft the Public Entertainments Licenses (Drugs Misuse) Bill in 1997, stating that "It gives the police fairly draconian powers to close down clubs, but we have to go a lot further."

Ironically, the subculture that had started out as a reaction to the mainstream, corporate nightclub scene, had been hijacked and sold back to the masses. This was McClubbing on a global scale: dance music would never be the same again.

"Night clubs are always about quality music with great DJs, and it's really hard to find something that appeals to my personal tastes on a regular basis . . . I'm not sure if the market could handle a weekly club like Cream again, but it has made me think whether we should do something on a more regular basis in Liverpool."

James Barton, founder of Cream

Superstar DJs, here we go!

With the rise of the superclub, it was perhaps inevitable that superstar DJs would follow.

At the height of the Madchester scene, two students at Manchester University—Ed Simons and Tom Rowlands—would go on to make some of the best dance albums ever. In 1992, Rowlands and Simons had begun DJ'ing at a small club in a Manchester pub, playing a selection of hip-hop, techno, and house. Initially dubbing themselves The 237 Turbo Nutters, they soon changed their name to The Dust Brothers, in honor of the US-based production duo.

In October 1992 they pressed 500 copies of "Song To The Siren" and tried to sell them in London dance-record stores—with little success. However, they had also sent a copy to Boy's Own co-founder Andrew Weatherall; he signed the duo to his Junior Boy's Own label, and released the track in May 1993.

In 1994, The Dust Brothers got a residency at the small but influential Heavenly Sunday Social Club at London's Albany pub, alongside Jon Carter. Set up by Heavenly Records, the club became the birthplace of Big Beat. In 1995, Simons and Rowlands had to change their name to The Chemical Brothers when the original Dust Brothers threatened to sue, hence the name of their first album: *Exit Planet Dust*.

With Heavenly's launching of further club nights at new locations in London, The Chemical Brothers took their first steps toward international stardom. Signing to Virgin Records, they released a string of hit albums, including *Dig Your Own Hole* and *Come With Us*. Despite their success, however, they remain as modest and media-shy as ever: "I just hope that our music triggers people's imaginations," said Simons in an interview in 2007. "It's absorbing, because it has got layers and textures . . ." Having been around for over ten years, the Chemicals wrily noted that the Ecstasy pills no longer have the desired effect on the track "The Pills Won't Help You Now," from their 2007 album *We Are the Night*.

In the mid-90s, the duo were befriended by an enthusiastic attendee at their DJ sets: Brighton's Norman Cook. Cook was no stranger to success himself, having already had several major hits under various guises. Then, in 1996, he released the dance album *Better Living Through Chemistry* under

the Fatboy Slim moniker. The album was a dance-floor smash, but it was his next album, *You've Come a Long Way, Baby*, released in 1998, that sent the Fatboy stratospheric. Previously, Cook had preferred to remain in the shadow of his music, but now he was reluctantly thrown into the media's glare and became a full-fledged "Superstar DJ."

Thanks to acts such as The Chemical Brothers, Fatboy Slim, Carl Cox, and others, the DJ had moved from anonymous warehouse deck-monkey and pirate radio spinner to superstardom, gaining respectability through record-producing, and the hosting of legitimate radio shows. DJs are now paid large fees to perform before huge audiences at events worldwide, and command as much respect as the musicians whose music they play. As one pundit noted, "DJs are the curators of the great musical collections, they sort through for the gems and play the best—like an exhibition."

Goa and full moon parties

As Ibiza became increasingly popular, and the superclubs increasingly soulless, the serious globetrotting raver was going further afield to find that unique "old-skool" vibe that was being destroyed by the lager-drinking mass-tourists who were quickly overrunning their beloved Balearic isle. The "hardcore" posse headed off on their quest to find somewhere they could "keep it real" and "fluffy." Some found it on the beaches of India and Thailand.

Typically, the ravers followed their parents' old hippie trail and ended up on southern India's Goan beaches. The resort was the perfect winter bolthole, maintaining a balmy temperature all year round. As with Ibiza, a hippie hardcore settled in Goa and experimented with drugs and music. The music that emerged from the scene in the early 90s would eventually come to be known as Goa trance, a music inspired mainly by industrial music such as Front Line Assembly, acid house such as The KLF's "What Time is Love?," and psychedelic rock along the lines of Ozric Tentacles and Steve Hillage. This eclectic mix was then further blended with local ethnic music and tribalesque drum patterns.

Goa trance parties usually occurred on the beach, sometimes in the middle of the forest, and occasionally in clubs. The local government tried, and failed, to commercialize the raves as had happened in Britain, but the ravers were having none of it. And as most promoters paid the local police baksheesh (a form of bribe), they could ensure they would be working free from any authoritarian pressures. The Goan parties had a definitive look about them, with lots of fluorescent painted clothing and tapestries glowing in the blacklight. The graphics were usually on a theme of "trippy," taking in anything from aliens, Hinduism, and mushrooms to shamanism and cutting-edge technology. Some people even erected shrines in front of the DJ stands, praising the shaman working his musical magic for the tribe.

The scene became huge with Israeli clubbers who traditionally went to Goa just before, or just after doing their military service, to let off steam. The Israeli government didn't like that, and actually sent a plane to bring its young people back, then arrested trance musicians Juno Reactor and Total Eclipse when they came to Israel to play.

In the mid-1990s, DJs such as Amsterdam Joey, Fred Disko, and Paul Oakenfold helped develop a mainstream style of trance outside Goa. In the US, in the mid-2000s, the popularity of Goa trance, or psytrance, grew with the warehouse party scene, and cities like San Francisco have seen an increase of warehouse parties since 2003, thanks to various Burning Man fundraiser raves.

By 2004, 400,000 foreign tourists visitors were coming to Goa. The dance scene in India was being swamped and it was time for the knapsack ravers to move on once more—this time to Thailand. First stop was Ko Samui, but the crowds soon followed there too. So, like the characters in Alex Garland's cult book *The Beach*, the roaming ravers set off to find their own little slice of heaven. They found it on the island of Ko Pha Ngan, where the spectacular beauty of the full moons tempted a few of the backpackers to stay and they started a small party in Haad Rin every month. The ravers mostly danced to psychedelic trance music tapes brought from Goa and the first Full Moon Party was improvised at a wooden disco next to the beach. As always, word of mouth spread the good news rather too quickly and suddenly 10,000 people were descending on to the beach every full moon. The music has diversified over the years to include drum and bass, house, and reggae. Local entrepreneurs have tried to cash in on the event with spin-off Half-Moon and Black Moon parties, with varying degrees of success.

Ravers regularly consumed copious amounts of Ecstasy, Yaa Baa (a.k.a. methamphetamine, or crystal meth), grass, and mushrooms at these events. But in 2002, the Thai government cracked down on illegal drugs at the parties, with 50,000-baht (£750/$1400) fines and jail sentences for foreigners found guilty of possession. Consequently, drug use has reduced at Full Moon parties. With no drugs and too many people it was time for the party to move on. But the world is shrinking, and finding that exclusive magical slice of ravers' paradise is becoming increasingly harder. Where they will end up next is anyone's guess.

Serotonin stories:
Mr. Greedy = Mr. Needy

In 2006, consultants from the addiction center at St. George's Medical School, London, published a report about a British man who was estimated to have consumed some 40,000 MDMA pills over a nine-year period, thus beating the unofficial previous lifetime consumption record of 2,000 pills.

The man, who was referred to only as "Mr. A," was 37 years old when the report was released; he had taken the drug between the ages of 21 and 30, but continued to suffer from severe physical and mental health side-effects seven years later. These included extreme memory problems, paranoia, hallucinations, and depression. He also suffered from painful stiffness of the muscles around his neck and jaw, which frequently prevented him from opening his mouth.

The report, in the journal *Psychosomatics*, stated that "Mr. A" had started by taking an average of five pills per weekend for the first two years. But he then gradually increased his intake until he was popping three and a half pills every day. Eventually, this hardest hardcore clubber of all time ended up taking a (literally) mind-blowing 25 pills every day—for a period of four years! Unsurprisingly, after collapsing several times at parties, "Mr. A" finally recognized that he had a problem, and he decided to stop taking Ecstasy.

Despite taking this sensible decision, "Mr. A" continued to feel the effects of the Ecstasy, and was bedridden. His condition worsened, and he began to experience recurrent tunnel vision and other problems, including hallucinations, paranoia, and muscle rigidity. Dr. Christos Kouimtsidis, the consultant psychiatrist at St. George's Medical School who treated "Mr. A" for five months, stated that "He came to us after deciding that he couldn't go on any more. He was having trouble functioning in everyday life."

The doctors reported that "Mr. A" was suffering from severe short-term memory problems of the sort usually only seen in lifelong alcoholics. Assessing the full range of damage he had wrought on his own brain was difficult, as his concentration and attention-span were so poor that he was unable to follow the basic tasks required by the tests.

"This was an exceptional case. His long-term memory was fine but he could not remember day-to-day things—the time, the day, what was in his supermarket trolley," said Dr. Kouimtsidis. "More worryingly, he did not seem aware himself that he had these memory problems."

Given that "Mr. A" had never previously suffered psychiatric problems, and that there was no history of mental illness in his family either, the doctors concluded that his unique condition was a direct result of his intense Ecstasy use. "Mr. A" was also a heavy user of cannabis—perhaps unsurprisingly, as he would have needed to take it to bring himself down after his Ecstasy binges. When he was encouraged to decrease the amount of weed he was smoking, his paranoia and hallucinations disappeared, and his sense of anxiety began to disperse. His memory and concentration problems, however, continued—forcing the doctors to conclude that they would be permanent.

When he was admitted to a specialist brain injury unit, and put on anti-psychotic medication, "Mr. A" eventually began to show some signs of improvement. Unfortunately, he discharged himself, dropped out of his rehab program, and started using cannabis again. The hospital lost all contact with "Mr. A." He is possibly still "out there" (in every sense of the phrase), but various efforts to track him down have failed. So, "Mr. A," if you are still among the living, we salute your stamina, sir, but please return to the hospital to get some help—now. And just occasionally, maybe, it would be a good idea to "just say no."

HARDCORE—YOU KNOW THE SCORE

07. Hardcore—you know the score

Ecstasy was about the music, but it was also about so much more. The drug somehow actively encouraged the brain to be more creative. People who had previously held back for fear of lack of talent threw their inhibitions to the wind and unleashed creativity in books, comics, art, and performance. Anything seemed to be possible. Ecstasy changed society in so many ways—large and small—in both the US and Britain. In Britain it impacted on the way people socialized at weekends (not least in that it led to the opening of all-night dance clubs), while in the US it prompted the youth to escape the confines of restrictive cities to rediscover the country's vast outdoors. But whereas Britain's small size enabled its youth easily to galvanize in one great movement, the vastness of the US meant that the thriving movements on the East and West Coasts, and in the Midwest and Florida, remained relatively separate. Ecstasy culture thus never quite captured the entire generation as a whole in the way that it did in Britain. A good indicator of the extent to which Ecstasy has nevertheless infiltrated everyday US life is the appearance of the Californian bumper sticker which jokingly warns of the dangers of getting too loved-up: "Don't get married for 6 months after Ecstasy."

The fashion . . . or lack of it

The years from the early to mid-80s were all about money—and about looking sharp, slick, and sleek. Suits were in, with rolled-up jacket sleeves, and espadrilles à la Crockett and Tubbs in *Miami Vice*. The girls had big hair and bigger shoulder pads, as promenaded in *Dynasty* and *Dallas*. The style was referred to as "power dressing," and rave railed against it. Ecstasy spelled the death of "style culture." As Nicky Trax observed in Jane Bussman's book, *Once in a Lifetime*: "In 1988 the dress code went to the toilet."

Unlike punk, new romanticism, or indeed any other previous youth movement, rave culture never really had a specific dress code or style. It was more anti-fashion than pro a particular style. Anything was accepted so long as one looked different from all the drones trying to look "suited and booted"

OPPOSITE, LEFT: THE SMILEY FACE WAS EVERYWHERE IN THE 80s, AND IT IS NOW—20 YEARS LATER—MAKING A FASHION COMEBACK. OPPOSITE, CENTER: IN RAVE FASHION ANYTHING WENT, AND USUALLY DID. GLOVES WERE PERENNIALLY POPULAR FOR WAVING AROUND. OPPOSITE, RIGHT: DUNGAREES, DE RIGUEUR FOR DITCH-DIGGERS, FARMERS—AND RAVERS.

on a Saturday night. Out of necessity, clothes had to be cool, comfortable, and loose-fitting—suitable for dancing in for long periods. "Keeping it baggy" was the thing. As the Happy Mondays sang in their classic track "Loose Fit," "Don't need no skin-tight in my wardrobe today . . ." Keeping their dress as simple as possible, the majority of ravers simply wore baggy Pepe jeans and psychedelic T-shirts. If there was anything that remotely constituted a uniform, it was the ubiquitous Smiley face tee.

Controversially, late 80s and early 90s styles have been making a comeback under the guise of Nu-Rave, which old-skool clubbers deride as premanufactured.

The Spiral Tribe

One of the most important developments to come out of rave culture is a sense of strong community. Even now, 20 years later, internet message boards are scattered with postings from survivors greeting each other, and reminiscing about the old days. That camaraderie is hard to explain to anyone who did not live through those wild, hedonistic days. "You get a sense of euphoria and a sense of togetherness," Human Traffic director Justin Kerrigan recalled. "That's the beautiful thing about the culture, that it brings together people from all different kinds of backgrounds and sexualities, class systems, and races through the music, but lets them express themselves as individuals. You don't get that in any other kind of culture, that feeling of unity. And even though the drug use is artificial, what's apparent is that everybody wants to feel like that naturally, to feel like that all the time, to feel comfortable with everyone . . ."

In 1990 Simon Harrison, determined to build on this sense of community, had the idea of organizing a series of free raves. He went on to set up an ongoing, rolling sound system that would criss-cross Britain, playing different venues every weekend. Its name (inspired by an ammonite fossil) was Spiral Tribe. Harrison's sound system eventually gathered a fluid, ever-changing entourage of followers, with new people replenishing the group as others moved on to new things. As MC Scallywag would regularly exclaim to the crowd: "We are not Spiral Tribe, you are all Spiral Tribe, it's you that makes the party happen."

When the British government stamped down on illegal raves with its draconian Criminal Justice Bill, Spiral Tribe decided to leave Britain for more conducive climes: they moved to France in 1992, and continued the partying across Europe. The tradition continues to this day, with sound systems all over the continent creating spontaneous open-air parties and festivals (teknivals) wherever and whenever possible; and as with CzechTek in the Czech Republic, many find themselves continually on the run from the police. In Britain, meanwhile, many free, touring party sound systems continue to "keep it real" for the old-skool crew; Brighton's The Positive Sound System, for example, was set up in 1992, (a year after Spiral Tribe was established) and it is still going strong 15 years later.

Rave Art: Mandelbrot sets and all that

The rave movement saw a renaissance of psychedelic art. Fueled by the advent of newly available digital technologies, rave developed a new graphic-art style influenced partly by 1960s psychedelic poster art, but also by graffiti art and 70s advertising. The rise of the home computer enabled budding creative types to begin experimenting with the new graphics programs—something entirely in keeping with the machine-created music behind it all.

Computer artists such as Brian Exton, for example, experimented with fractal imagery, using complex programming to create detailed and visually stunning geometric shapes and patterns. The bright colors and intricate patterns were perfect to stare at while on MDMA, and fractals soon permeated other areas of popular culture. Endless fractal-themed postcards and T-shirts were produced and no student's room would have been complete without a Mandelbrot Set poster on the wall.

"Magic Eye" posters and books also became hugely popular—these featured hidden images in a mass of seemingly meaningless computer-generated patterns known as "autostereograms." If stared at for long enough, and in the right way, the viewer would see 3-D images. Of course, all these "mind games" appealed to ravers, who were already well down the road to experimenting with perceived reality.

Other psychedelic artists, such as Alex Grey and Robert Venosa, steadfastly devoted themselves to more traditional "analog" methods of painting, but also saw an increased interest in their work.

On a more theatrical level there was the Mutoid Waste Company, an arts/performance group/post-punk arts collective who created vast scrap-metal statues and sculptures and threw huge parties. The greatest moment for these squatter-activist traveler artists came in Berlin in 1998, when they created a giant "Stonehenge" out of old Eastern Bloc tanks in time for the city's reinstatement as the capital of a reunited Germany.

This rave-inspired artistic expression applied across the board, in all media, from movies and TV to comics—and, of course, to the flyers advertising the next big event.

ABOVE: THE MUTOID WASTE COMPANY BUILD ONE OF THEIR FIRST "CARHENGE" INSTALLATIONS AT THE BRITISH GLASTONBURY FESTIVAL.

Rave Art: the flyers

Invariably many flyer designers co-opted comic book imagery and simply cut out pictures they liked, or felt represented the mood or tone of their rave. Artists such as Brian Bolland and the British sci-fi comic, *2000 AD*, were frequently culled for pictures. As Jane Bussman wrote, "Why were rave flyers so embarrassing? Probably because they were very upfront about what was on offer—mind expansion, peace and love . . . " Unfortunately that often involved relying on pictures of fairies, deep space, and other sci-fi and fantasy-related "found" images "borrowed" from *Heavy Metal* magazine. Other promoters were inspired by the poster and flyer art of such San Francisco-based artists of the 60s as Rick Griffin, Victor Moscoso, and Robert Williams.

Some of the better flyers were produced by Philip Sallon, who preferred to call them "invites." Boy's Own Productions had published their own fanzine, so their artwork was superior, too. They took the Clockwork Orange logo and gave it their own unique twist, using their instantly recognizable black-and-white 1920s street orphan boy and his pet dog for one of their flyers.

As time moved on, and the big superclubs such as Pacha, Ministry of Sound, and Cream started taking over, the flyers became more sophisticated and better designed—but simultaneously colder and more heartless. More corporate. For the quality that had made the early flyers so embarrassing—their homemade appearance—was also what made them so endearing. Well, probably: in Bussman's words, "Either that or they were just shit."

Crazy comics: Russell, Bastard Bunny, and crew

Just as the first Summer of Love sparked off the underground comix movement in San Francisco in the 60s, so there was a smaller comic scene tied to rave culture. Admittedly it was a lot smaller than the previous movement, and most of the comic strips were derogatory about acid house, but ravers bought them anyway, as they were more than willing to laugh at themselves. More often than not, acid casualties coming down from a weekend of raving, or even still "on one," could be found wandering around comic stores convinced that the comic characters were talking directly to them.

Inspired by the work of Gilbert Shelton's creation the Fabulous Furry Freak Brothers—which was undergoing a revival in popularity as a new generation discovered it—Peter Loveday started publishing Big Bang Comics. His strips told the Saga of a Peaceful Man—Russell, a well-meaning hippie who traveled to all the festivals and examined the growing sub-cultures that rave was throwing up, such as the burgeoning traveler community.

At the same time, at the beginning of the 90s, David Anderson was visiting all the comic stores in London trying to persuade them to stock his self-published title *Bastard Bunny*. The drug-snorting, violent, club-going, psychotic rabbit had all the elements of an underground hit. Interestingly, "BB"—as his mates knew him—was more of a backlash to the whole loved-up culture; dressed in jeans and braces, with Doc Marten boots, he looked more like a skinhead. He hated posers, techno, and taxi drivers. But BB's love of weed and choice of friends—including Toot Toucan (a cocaine-snorting, acid-taking tropical bird)—meant that he regularly came into contact with club culture.

Bastard Bunny was written by Anderson and drawn by a variety of artists including Jiouxleigh Jacobs, Martyn Smith, and Pol Sigerson. The humorous writing and simple yet effective art meant that shops regularly asked for restocks.

To help promote the comic Anderson began selling T-shirts too, and these (briefly) became hip anti-fashion rave wear in London. Ironically, this subsidiary business eventually became more successful than the comic itself. When Anderson created a T-shirt pastiche of the Warner Brothers logo with "BB" instead of "WB," self-professed comic fan, stand-up comedian, and actor Bill Bailey bought several and started wearing them on stage and on TV.

OPPOSITE, TOP: COVER TO KNOCKABOUT'S ACID HEAD ARNIE COLLECTION, WHICH WAS WRITTEN AND DRAWN BY ANTHONY SMITH. OPPOSITE, BOTTOM: VIZ MAGAZINE'S RAVEY DAVEY GRAVY "GETS ON ONE"—IN THE FOREGROUND—AS HE DANCES ON THE COVER TO NO.76.

Many people thought he'd had them made specially, but as he explained in a 2004 interview, "This actually stands for a comic strip called *Bastard Bunny*, a cute, lovable rabbit: he's an underground DJ with a speed problem. When I met the guy who does the comic strip he seemed quite cool about me wearing the shirt because it's free advertising for him."

Virgin Books collected all of BB's adventures into a single volume in 1998 called, *Don't You Know Who I Am!* The cover showed BB and Toot trying to get past a club doorman, a recurring joke throughout his misadventures.

Crazy comics: Ravey Davey Gravy and Acid Head Arnie

Many humorous comics in Britain latched onto the whole rave culture. *Viz* was an adult humor anthology that was fast becoming a national British phenomenon in 1987, just as the acid house scene was taking off, and many ravers read the comic. It soon developed into a parody of classic children's comics such as *The Beano* and *The Dandy*, but with adult themes and characters who swore, smoked, drank alcohol, and "shagged." *Viz*'s cast ranged from The Fat Slags and Sid the Sexist to the "mental" clubber Ravey Davey Gravy.

Ravey Davey was a Smurf-hatted, baggy-panted jerk who continually mistook the noise of reversing trucks, police sirens, pneumatic drills, or indeed any repetitive noise for the latest block-rocking beat. His eternal quest for Ecstasy and other drugs led him into all sorts of surreal situations, usually involving terrible puns. When he's asked if he'd like to "Score some grass," Ravey leaps at the chance, only to discover he's been asked to judge a lawnmower competition . . .

Ravey continuously spouted endless, meaningless catchphrases taken from the club floor: "Oowa! Kickin' it large! Give us the bass in m'face!"; "Banging!"; "Let's 'ave it!," and so on. Like all truly ridiculous characters, he was blissfully unaware of his own absurdity. Drawn by *Viz* mainstay Simon Thorp, Ravey was a regular feature in the comic in the mid-to-late 90s but then disappeared as the rave scene died down, and was assimilated into regular club-going. But he remained a favorite with clubbers and his name was adopted by many as their own nickname. Davey never went away completely, and made a brief return in *Viz* in 2002.

Viz spawned endless imitators, including *Zit*, *Spit*, *Oink*, and *Brain Damage*, and so it was no surprise that another cartoon raver would emerge in the pages of *Zit*. "Acid Head Arnie" was written and drawn by Anthony Smith and told the everyday story of a young man whose sole aim in life was to take LSD and go to raves. The strip was later published in *Brain Damage* as well; in 1994, Knockabout released a collection, following it up three years later with another, entitled *Acid Head: Arnie's Bad Trip*. While the art and writing was superior, poor old Arnie never quite grabbed the public's attention as Ravey Davey had done.

Largin' lit: Irvine Welsh, Disco Biscuits et al.

The literary world wasn't very far behind the rave scene, and when *Trainspotting* author Irvine Welsh turned his attention to MDMA, it was no real surprise. He had been a fan of house music for years and had even worked as a DJ, promoter, and producer.

Ecstasy: Three Tales of Chemical Romance was published in 1996 and became Welsh's most high-profile work since that infamous tale about Edinburgh heroin addicts. *Ecstasy* consists of three unconnected novellas: the first, "Lorraine Goes To Livingston," is a bawdy satire of classic British romance novels; the second, "Fortune's Always Hiding," is a revenge story involving thalidomide; and the third, "The Undefeated," is a subtle romance between a young woman dissatisfied with the confines of her suburban life and an aging clubber. In the latter, Welsh's narration portrayed both characters with surprising warmth, and the story avoided easy, pro-Ecstasy conclusions. As *Spike Magazine* noted, "Welsh smoothly demonstrates his belief in the liberating power of dance culture. Most interestingly, he avoids the easy route of claiming utopia. If drugs can liberate you, then they can as easily ruin you." Having been turned into a stage play, a movie version of *Ecstasy* was being filmed in 2007, directed by Rob Heydon and starring Richard E. Grant and Billy Boyd.

Welsh also contributed to Sarah Champion's 1997 anthology *Disco Biscuits* (the title is slang for Ecstasy). This paean to club culture featured contributions from numerous writers, including Dean Cavanagh's wittily twisted "Mile High Meltdown" and Welsh's "State of The Party." Mancunian editor Champion had been at the heart of acid house, and had gone to the Haçienda for the first time

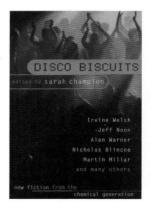

aged just 15. By the time she was 20, she had already documented the Manchester music scene for *NME*, had her own weekly column in the *Manchester Evening News*, and gained a reputation as something of a "wild child." She then became involved in London's electronic music world and traveled the globe writing about club culture for various dance-music publications. Her "chemical fiction" collection *Disco Biscuits* became Britain's best-selling fiction anthology of all time, racking up sales of 60,000 in a few weeks.

In 1997, author, teacher, and free thinker Douglas Rushkoff produced another seminal slice of E-culture fiction with *The Ecstasy Club*. The book chronicled the lives of a group of young, hypertalented idealists—the self-named Ecstasy Club—who discover an abandoned piano factory in Oakland, in which they create a round-the-clock rave the likes of which the Bay Area has never seen before. They also make the factory a base camp in their search for a method of time travel that combines computer wizardry, esoteric spirituality, and mind-altering substances. Fellow scribe Jeff Noon wrote that "Rushkoff turns his extensive knowledge of the cyberscene into a brilliant fictional account of the rise and fall of a rave club. His work rides the fractal edge between hippy values and the new wave of technoshamanism, to chronicle the commercialization of the Underground."

OPPOSITE: THE COVER TO SARAH CHAMPION'S BEST-SELLING ANTHOLOGY, *DISCO BISCUITS*.
BELOW, LEFT: THE JACKET OF DOUGLAS RUSHKOFF'S 1997 NOVEL, *THE ECSTASY CLUB*.
BELOW, CENTER: WELSH'S SHORT STORY COLLECTION, *ECSTASY: THREE TALES OF CHEMICAL ROMANCE*, WITH ITS ICONIC COVER DESIGN.
BELOW, RIGHT: SCOTTISH WRITER IRVINE WELSH HAS BUILT A HIGHLY SUCCESSFUL CAREER WRITING ABOUT RECREATIONAL DRUG USE.

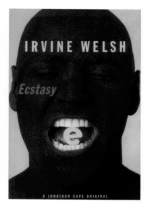

There are, of course, endless books that feature Ecstasy-taking, and club culture—far too many to list here. But Ecstasy's impact has been even greater in another field of the arts: cinema.

Mashed movies: Wasted and Coming Down

Arguably the best TV show ever made about dance culture was *A Short Film About Chilling*, which was shot in Ibiza in 1990, just before the island became famous worldwide for its club culture. The documentary followed a group of DJs, bands, and clubbers intent on "losing it" in the island's legendary nightclubs, which are described as being like "Disneyland for the club-goer." The viewer will have endless entertainment spotting the faces of future supermodels, star DJs, designers, and pop stars among the motley crowds featured raving or chilling at the now legendary Café del Mar.

Released in 1996, the Belgian/Dutch movie *Naar de Klote!* (which translates literally as "To the bollocks!" or "To get wasted") was one of the first to address issues relating to Ecstasy use and clubbing. When twentysomething innocents Jacqui and Martijn move to Amsterdam and immerse themselves in the intense, drug-laden underground club scene, life turns out to be far more complicated, difficult, and dangerous than they bargained for. But despite the trials and tribulations the couple undergo, the movie is surprisingly pro-drugs.

ABOVE, LEFT: A SCENE FROM THE MOVIE *NAAR DE KLOTE!* FEATURING THE ACTRESSES FEM VAN DER ELZEN AND TYGO GERNANDT IN THE AMSTERDAM RAVE SCENE.

ABOVE, RIGHT: THE MOVIE POSTER FOR THE BELGIAN/DUTCH PRODUCTION, *NAAR DE KLOTE!*

OPPOSITE, LEFT: COMEDY ACTOR STEVE COOGAN PLAYS HACIENDA FOUNDER, TONY WILSON, IN THE BRITISH MOVIE *24-HOUR PARTY PEOPLE*.

OPPOSITE, RIGHT: THE HAPPY MONDAYS AS PORTRAYED IN *24-HOUR PARTY PEOPLE*. AS STEVE COOGAN (PLAYING TONY WILSON) SAYS IN THE MOVIE, "EVERY BAND NEEDS ITS OWN SPECIAL CHEMISTRY. AND BEZ WAS A VERY GOOD CHEMIST."

Director Ian Kerkhof explained: "I wanted show both sides, the bad and the good . . . I don't believe in a convenient 'Just say no' message, and neither does my audience."

Another director who knew his audience was Matt Win, who made *Coming Down* (1997). The short movie shows a group of friends returning after a "pilled-up" night out to chill in a friend's flat.

Mashed movies: Human Traffic to 24-Hour Party People

The British movie industry has made many films about clubbing. And one of the funniest is Michael Winterbottom's 2002 exploration of the Madchester scene and the Haçienda: *24-Hour Party People* (the title was taken from a Happy Mondays track).

The movie follows Mancunian legend Tony Wilson (hilariously played by Steve Coogan) who—after seeing a seminal Sex Pistols gig—is inspired to set up a record label, Factory Records, sign Joy Division (who go on to become New Order), then James and the Happy Mondays. The legendary tale of

music, sex, drugs, and larger-than-life characters explores one of the most famous dance clubs in the world. As Wilson/Coogan states in the movie: "And tonight something equally epoch-making is taking place. See? They're applauding the DJ. Not the music, not the musician, not the creator, but the medium. This is it. The birth of rave culture. The beatification of the beat. The dance age. This is the moment when even the white man starts dancing. Welcome to Manchester." Or more simply, as the Happy Mondays' maraca-shaking dancer Bez says, "Can I offer anybody, like, the best drug experience they ever had?"

Another impressive movie that captured the essence of clubbing was set in the Cardiff, Wales, club scene in the 90s and was writer/director Justin Kerrigan's first feature. *Human Traffic* tells the tale of five best friends—Jip, Lulu, Nina, Koop, and Moff—escaping their McJobs, partying throughout one weekend, and how they cope with their relationships and personal demons. British newspaper *The Guardian* called it "the last great film of the 90s," and it is packed with classic scenes familiar to any clubber, from the preparations for clubbing, through the Ecstasy-induced highs and inane conversations, to the booze-laden comedown on Saturday morning.

Kerrigan, who was only 25 years old when the movie was released, wrote from the heart: "I've always been into clubs. I used to basically live in clubs. A lot of my friends are DJs and they used to put on raves, outdoor raves, and such." After Radio One's DJ Pete Tong was shown a rough cut, he quickly became the movie's music supervisor and champion. The movie also saw notable guest appearances by DJ Carl Cox as nightclub owner Pablo Hassan, and legendary Welsh cannabis smuggler and author Howard Marks as himself, explaining the etiquette of dope smoking.

There were rumors that Kerrigan fell out with his producer, Allan Niblo, during the shoot, and that the director wasn't consulted on the re-edit of the movie on DVD, *Human Traffic Remixed*. But despite that, it remains much-loved by clubbers.

Fittingly the British première of the movie took place in a giant chill-out tent at the Homelands dance festival in front of 200 slightly jaded dance casualties. It was, naturally, a hit.

'Stunning, Sharp, Funny and Mind-blowingly Good'

'A Riot of a Comedy'
★ ★ ★ ★ ★

'Absolute Genius'
★ ★ ★ ★

it's all gone pete tong

When you can't hear the look very different

"The weekend has landed. All that exists now is clubs, drugs, pubs and parties. I've got 48 hours off from the world, man. I'm gonna blow steam out my head like a screaming kettle."

Jip in *Human Traffic* (1999)

Mashed movies: It's All Gone Pete Tong, Go, Groove, and Rolling

Following on from the cult success of 1999's *Human Traffic*, producer Allan Niblo wanted to make a more in-depth movie about the ever-growing club scene. In 2004, he hired Canadian director Michael Dowse to put together *It's All Gone Pete Tong*. Dowse knew nothing about clubbing, so he spent a year hanging out in all the superclubs in London, Ibiza, and Miami undertaking "research."

The movie starred Paul Kaye as arrogant superstar DJ Frankie Wilde, a hysterically accurate amalgamation of every bad habit DJs are known for, from bad teeth to the rockstar partying lifestyle. The "mocumentary" follows Wilde in his hedonistic life at the height of his fame on Ibiza. With a record contract in hand, he lives an opulent life performing at the hottest nightclubs and living in a gorgeous villa with his trophy-model wife Sonya. But things start to go wrong when Frankie starts going deaf—every DJ's worst nightmare—and he has to revaluate his life. "Maybe I should write a book," he muses at one point. "That might take years, though. Perhaps a pamphlet or brochure . . ." Frankie's battle with drug addiction manifests itself in the form of a 7ft-tall "coke badger," which he constantly fights with.

"Pot and beer fuck you up; this [E] enhances you. It gives you a heightened sense of awareness, especially touch, a feeling of connection . . . openness . . . honesty. It is just like being a kid."

Cliff in *Groove* (2000)

LEFT: THE MAN THE MOVIE WAS NAMED FOR—THE LEGENDARY DJ AND PRODUCER, PETE TONG.
FAR, LEFT: A SCENE FROM THE 2000 MOVIE *GROOVE*. A CLUBBER SHOWS HE HAS BALLS, ALBEIT ONLY ONE. BUT IT'S BIG, AND GLITTERING.

Pete Tong not only had his name in the title—London rhyming slang for "It's all gone wrong"—but also took a small cameo role, playing himself interviewing a totally out-of-his-head Frankie. Having worked with Allan Niblo as music supervisor on *Human Traffic*, Tong came on board as executive producer for his eponymous movie. He also created three tracks for it, working with music supervisor Lol Hammond. Throughout the movie there are guest appearances by top DJs, playing themselves. These include Carl Cox and Paul van Dyk, who states at one point, "Frankie was definitely one of the best. He had his very own style, his very own momentum with the crowd. I don't think that anyone else did it his way."

The movie encapsulated everything that dance music is about, but while set in the Ibiza club scene it went far beyond the "pills, thrills, and belly aches" of a Saturday night clubbing. Hilarious in parts, dark and bitter in others, it won many international awards.

The US has had its fair share of Ecstasy-inspired movies as well, including *Go*—about a botched major Ecstasy deal—and 2000's *Groove*.

Groove tells the story of two brothers at an illegal Saturday night rave with 200 people in an abandoned warehouse. The world of the San Francisco underground dance scene is explored effectively, and the movie also features esteemed DJ John Digweed as the rave's headline act. All the other DJs who play throughout the movie are notable West Coast DJs, including Polywog, Forest Green, and WishFM. "Pot and beer fuck you up; this enhances you," says a sage-like Cliff in *Groove*. "It gives you a heightened sense of awareness, especially touch, a feeling of connection . . . openness . . . honesty. It is just like being a kid."

Rolling (2007) transferred the action from San Francisco down the coast to LA, and comes across like an Ecstasy-fueled version of Robert Altman's *Short Cuts*. A med student, teenage runaway, lawyer, drag queen, high-school basketball player, drug dealer, and teacher all intersect in the underground party scene. Shot in a documentary style, *Rolling* captures the essence of Ecstasy culture, exposing the delicate balance of relationships and responsibilities experienced while being off your head.

Other movies that touched on US Ecstasy culture included *Party Girl*, *Rave*, and *Party Monster*, but these productions took a more moralistic point of view, and focused more on the negative aspects of clubbing and MDMA consumption.

Brighton's Big Beat Boutique

In the beginning of the 1990s in Britain, several locally based electronic music genres began to intersect in the London Club scene, as with the aforementioned Heavenly Social and pioneer DJs, The Chemical Brothers. Sampling existing tracks, and looping elements, became an integral part of what became known as "Big Beat." The unique sound was generated by a melange of distorted, compressed breakbeats at moderate tempos (usually 90 to 140bpm—slower than most dance tracks at the time), along with acidic synthesizer lines and heavy jazz loops, punctuated with punkish-style vocals and driven by intense, distorted bass lines with conventional pop and techno

"This was not an ordinary night . . . This was bigger than anything I could have imagined. We love to party in Brighton but this was really something else."

Norman Cook on Big Beach Boutique II

song structures. Into this hodge podge went everything from Rock, Funk, Industrial, Jazz, Acid House, Hip-Hop, and Trance, as highlighted by one of Fatboy Slim's earliest tracks, "Punk to Funk."

The sound caught on, and a wide variety of acts were put under the moniker of "Big Beat" including Bentley Rhythm Ace, Death in Vegas and David Holmes.

Other notable acts were Apollo 440, The Midfield General, Freddy Fresh, Groove Armada, Lo Fidelity Allstars, Propellerheads, Space Raiders, Scanty Sandwich, and The Wiseguys and many artists signed to London's Wall Of Sound and Brighton's Skint labels.

Meanwhile Norman Cook (Fatboy Slim), inspired by Felix Da Housecat, The Chemical Brothers, and Carl Cox, was DJ'ing regularly at the Concorde club in Brighton on its Big Beat Boutique night, which had been launched in 1996 by Gareth Hansome. In 2001 he decided to host a free rave on the beach with an audience of 45,000 locals. It was a huge success and a follow-up concert was planned for the following year. Unfortunately the previous year's event had been shown on TV, and on July 13, 2002, some 250,000 people turned up from all over the country. Although the city was overwhelmed by the crowds, the event was considered a huge success. However, fearing that they could not cope with another similar event, the authorities banned Fatboy Slim from holding any beach parties for another four and a half years.

In 2007 Brighton police finally relinquished the ban, but this time tickets were made available only to Brighton residents. The gig kicked off with DJ David Guetta, and took place on a wet, cold New Year's Day, 2007. Yet despite all this, 20,000 fans still turned up to dance in the rain, indicating the draw that Cook and dance music still had.

The three massive gigs provided proof that there is still life in dance music; and that a second generation—who were not even born when Acid House first emerged—have now taken up the mantle of their elder brothers, sisters, or even parents. With talk of "New Rave," "electroclash," and other related dance movements emerging all the time, the next generation are maintaining the right and freedom to party, and to experience the potential for a happier world. Generation Ecstasy has, indeed, "Come a long way, Baby."

OPPOSITE, LEFT: THE FIRST BIG BEACH BOUTIQUE, IN 2001, WAS AFFECTIONATELY KNOWN AS "NORMSTOCK." THE FOLLOWING YEAR 250,000 PEOPLE FROM AS FAR AWAY AS SCOTLAND DESCENDED ON THE CITY ON ENGLAND'S SOUTH COAST.

OPPOSITE, RIGHT: NORMAN COOK, OR FATBOY SLIM, PLEASES THE CROWDS IN HIS HOMETOWN OF BRIGHTON IN ENGLAND.

Serotonin stories:
Clubbing for the post-e generation

Almost uniquely among all recreational drugs, Ecstasy seems to have its own self-regulatory system. That is, after using it for a while most people never recapture the initial "breakthrough" experience again and consequently give up taking it. As with most shamanistic rituals, the drug is the signpost to experiencing a different reality and shouldn't be relied upon solely. Consequently, the majority of the older generation of clubbers have become jaded about the drug and have stopped taking E, or at least do it very infrequently. This anonymous clubber expresses feelings held by many of his peers:

"I first became aware of the dance scene in the summer of 1991 in Orlando, Florida. I was almost 21 at that time and was a patron of many clubs, mostly to meet with friends, do a little dancing, and to drink sociably.

"As I spent time in the clubs and the rave scene, I learned of the different types of drugs that were readily available just by asking (it was easy to do then). Acid (LSD) was my first experiment (I have also smoked pot on a regular basis over the years)—that was a blast! After dosing several hundred hits, I learned the effects were sporadic at best due to varied potency and improper handling.

"My next experiment was with mushrooms, they grow wildly in the region of the US that I am from and were a fun, natural high that was easily dosed and absolutely FREE! I must mention that before I ever went out looking for mushrooms (and all the drugs I have tried), I did research both at the local public library and with some friends who had been doing drugs for years to make sure I was picking the correct ones.

"The next chemical I chose to try was Ecstasy. As I started my use of this 'Love Drug,' I found a new and wonderful experience that I had never before been able to achieve, either sober or with any other drug.

"After about six years of use, and a lot of time, money, two years of legal problems, and the loss of several good friends (may they rest in peace),

"With any drug you may decide to try, please know what you are taking, and know the environment you are going into."

I decided that it was time for me to stop. I have had a lot of great times that will forever remain deeply inbedded in my soul from the use and sharing of Ecstasy and other drugs, but there were a lot of bad times also.

"With any drug you may decide to try, please know what you are taking, and know the environment you are going into. I am now more than two years 'sober' and still enjoy the music scene as much as I did when I was using . . . well, maybe not quite as much as when I was on Ecstasy, but the music is the main reason why I ever started dancing in the first place, and the reason I keep going back.

"I want people to know that you don't have to check out of reality just to have a good time in the club/dance scene, the music is a trip in itself. Remembering the music is always better than not remembering the trip, and do it safe!"

Which, all in all, is just another way of saying "Keep it real!"

Index

Page references in *italics* indicate illustration captions

Acknowledgments

More than any book I've ever written, this has been a real team effort. Although my name is on the cover, thanks must go to Will, Katie, Rob and Paul for helping ensure my meanderings make sense, and for pulling together the amazing images that fill this tome. Massive thanks also to the gentlemanly Douglas Rushkoff for contributing his foreword, and to Julie Holland and Cynthia Fowles at Inner Traditions for allowing us to adapt and re-use their text. Also, a huge thank you for the kind words and support from Skint Records and Norman Cook— Mate, you've been a true inspiration to me for years, keep it up! This also is for Danny Rampling, Johnnie Walker, Nicky Holloway and Paul Oakenfold, without whom there would not even have been a rave scene to write about! To my long-suffering family and friends (as always) and my old Ecstasy Club: Art, Paul, Angelos, Simon, Ellie, Helen, Annabel, Phil Silcock and the entire Brighton Love Lounge crew—lots of love to you all, wherever you are. And to everybody I met and spoke to during the course of writing this book who offered help, advice and material: you've proved that the ties of the "Old Skool" are still strong, and that everyone is still keeping the spirit of 87 and 88 alive. "Nice one, Fellas!"

Editors' acknowledgments: Thanks to EcstasyData.org for supplying most of the photographs in the Catalog of Pills.

Photo credits

The editors wish to thank the following for granting permission to reproduce the images featured in the book. Every effort has been made to contact copyright holders, though the publishers would welcome any further information so that future editions may be updated.

Frankie Bones: 131L. Mike Conroy: 27. Corbis/Ted Streshinsky: 17; Scott Houston/Sygma: 18, 42, 46, 128; Bettmann: 25L; Deborah Feingold: 32; Reuters: 47L; Brenda Ann Kenneally: 49; Robert Holmes: 82R; Lynn Goldsmith: 93L; Jeffery Allan Salter/SABA: 135B; Sygma: 136L; Kevin Lamarque/Reuters: 141R; Yves Herman/Reuters: 142. Steve Double. Courtesy Random House: 171R. Drop Bass Network: 134T, 134B, 135 [Art: John Kuzich]. EcstasyData.org: 64-71 [except Alligator, Batman, Durex]. EcstasyData.org is a project which conducts laboratory testing of the contents of street Ecstasy tablets and publishes the results online. Everynight Images/Debbie Bragg: 89L; Jamie Baker: 145, 146R, 148. Getty Images/Hulton Archive: 14T; Time Life Pictures: 25R, 29, 141L; Michael Ochs Archives: 74R, 81T; Matthew Naythons: 85; Ian McKell/Reportage: 152. Bill Hardy: 81. © Estate of Keith Haring: 84. Hyperreal.org: 24B, 88T, 92, 104, 106TR, 107, 108, 132, 167 [4 x BL]. Freetekno.cz: 121L, 121R. iStockphoto/Christian Anthony: 41R; Sebastian Kaulitzki: 41L; Oleg Prikhodko: 51B; Domenico Leoci: 73; Spectral Design: 158; 165R. The Kobal Collection/Channel 4: 173L, 173R; Metrodome/Irish Screen: 175L; True West Films/Vertigo Films: 175R; 415 Prod/Groove LLC: 176L. Johannes Kroemer: 55B. Library of Congress, Washington, D.C.: 10. Alan Lodge [Tash]: 166. PA Photos/David Karp: 74L; Yui Mok: 178L; PA Photos: 178R. Park Street Press, an imprint of Inner Traditions International, Rochester, VT [www.InnerTraditions.com]: 55T. © Tina Paul [Fifibear.com]: 76, 77. Courtesy Plexifilm: 78, 79BL, 79BR. PYMCA/Pav Modelski: 38; Jason Manning: 43L; Rob Watkins: 43R; Tristan O'Neill: 44, 162L; Adrian Fisk: 45R; David Swindells: 47R, 96L, 97, 102, 106L, 106BR, 109, 161L, 161M, 161R, 162R; Peter J Walsh: 113R; Paul Massey: 117; Dean Chalkley: 146L. Rex Features/Eugene Adebari: 30L; Images: 31; 89R; Iris Honold: 93R; David Graves: 94; Richard Young: 96R; Nicholas Bailey: 118; Sipa Press: 131R; Roger Sargent: 150L; Jonathan Hordle: 176R. Courtesy Roland: 83. Ian Tilton Photography [www.iantilton.net]: 88B, 113L, 114. Trax Records: 81B.